Diary of the Damned

It Happened On A Sunday

BARBARA ALLEN STOVALL

Queen B

This book is dedicated to my four precious faces.

TABLE OF CONTENTS

PREFACE

I AM A plain and simple woman. I can be easy-going or complex depending on the subject or situation. I don't have any college degrees, Trade School Certifications or even a high school diploma. However, what I do possess is a talent that has aided, inspired and saved plenty of folk from agony and self-destruction during their darkest and most pressing hour. It has even cost me some family, quite a few acquaintances and friends, too. My skill is the use of words. It doesn't matter if I speak with my voice or write on paper, those in my path take heed to what I have too say.. Many of the things I reveal are from my heart stemming from some personal experiences, or perhaps from related advice from others. And yes, sometimes it even comes from God, Himself. It's a great joy when others can relate to me because sometimes being me can be hard and lonely.

Quite often, we allow pain to enter our lives freely and willingly, despite the warning signs. All too frequently, we try to prove our worth to others. We get so caught up in trying to please others that we lose sight of who we are. We find ourselves morphing into something that we never set out to become. On the contrary, a small number of us are able to come back to ourselves after we reboot ourselves with hope. There's an abundance of us that feel lost and deserted while on a search for an unconditional love. This thing, this need to be accepted and loved without restrictions or judgment eats away at our soul like a cancer.

I don't know much about a lot of things: but what I do know is a multitude of humans proclaiming to be in love aren't in love at all. They are consumed with something called obsession, but they would never admit it. I know because I have obsessed a time or two about people, places and things. All that changed when I met someone that saw my natural beauty and true nature. He made me become aware that loving me first was necessary in order for happiness to always be the core of my existence. I would like to encourage those who think they can't break away from their obsession, regardless of what it is, to know that although it may seem hopeless and you may feel helpless and victimized to a brink of demerit, you are not alone.

Hopefully, my tale can help you know that all is never lost and there are really rainbows after the storms! After all, always and forever are two very different things!

PROLOGUE

AS WE GO through the process of childhood to adulthood, we never know what or who is lurking, waiting to grab our attention. We grow up blissfully dreaming about Santa Claus and the Tooth Fairy, sadly still aware that the boogie man is coming to get you if you don't do right. Our innocence is always being watched carefully by some one that we'd never think would offend our precious value. There are a great deal of us that may escape terror. But for the few who can't, no matter the age, race, or gender are forced into suffocation. They are in dire need of oxygen, because they're choking off of emptiness and confusion. Some of us learn how to breathe again, only when someone comes along as stubborn as we are, commit themselves into forcing us to understand that their help is required for us to become better. No matter what our history, there will always be two sides to every story. Here is mine.

THE ARRIVAL

THEIR CRIES WERE synchronized along with the thunderstorm that was wreaking havoc on the city for the last several hours. The heavy raindrops pounded away at the already battered old rooftop of the state's only free hospital, causing an electrical surge which immediately kicked on the emergency generator to the relief of the staff and patients, alike. The storm not only caused severe flooding, but the ghastly winds knocked down trees and power lines all over the city, causing many folk to leave their cars stranded in the middle of the streets and on the medians. Finally, with the break of dawn, the rain ceased and the torment of two particular young girls. *They'd suffered side by side, enduring long hours of grueling and excruciating pain that came from being in labor. Both gave birth five minutes apart:* One had a girl, the other a boy. Although they experienced the same blood, sweat and tears of bringing life into the world together and briefly shared a room during their recovery, the two never bothered to disclose a thing about themselves to one another. Nope, not even their names.

FOURTEEN YEARS LATER

THE THIRD FRIDAY of July in 1983 was an extremely hot and wind-less day. Because we lived in the South, it wasn't that unusual for the temperature to be high during the months of summer. But that day, was different. It was only 7:00am in the morning and it **felt like hell had somehow surfaced above** on **earth**. The three air conditioners and six box fans had to push extra hard to cool my family's eight room house. Despite the heatwave, I headed downstairs to the kitchen to fix a pot of grits for my siblings, along with a fresh pot of coffee for my daddy. After this was done, I braved the heat by heading out the side door to the bakery around the corner to get my pops a fresh baked loaf of French-bread for his breakfast. Upon returning back from my routine errand, I completed my dreaded chores, then, woke my mama, so we could discuss church business. She and I were in charge of our church's Annual Sunday School Celebration taking place on the last Sunday of August.

After countless attempts of re-calculating our financial ledger for the upcoming event, Mama and I became frustrated because we still needed a significant amount of money to make the event successful. We were doing all we could to raise money by having bake sales and raffles. Even the donations we were receiving didn't seem to account for much. Our most stressing concerns were the balance owed for the trophies and the need for a professional printer. We were focused on ways to remedy these two problems for most of the morning, yet we couldn't come up with any new solutions. Becoming aggravated we both decided to take a break from our upsetting dilemmas.

Later on during the afternoon, I was up in my bedroom relaxing across the bed, when an idea binged in my head. I hurried downstairs and found mama lying in bed on the phone, talking to Sister Price about our shortcomings. I anxiously beckoned her to cut her call short, so, I could reveal the plan I thought could possibly resolve our printing situation. She sat and listened attentively to my suggestion while drinking her coke and snacking on Oreo cookies. Once I was done with the details of my plan, she excitedly nodded her head up and down stating my idea was brilliant. I instructed her to cross her fingers and hope for the best, as I picked up the phone and nervously dialed the number of my old pal. While the phone was ringing, I momentarily felt a little ashamed of how long we had been out of touch; it had has been nearly three years. When he answered the other end of the phone, it was like we never stopped communicating. After having a brief conversation with my estranged friend, I hung up the receiver and began jumping up and down, because I was excited that my friend was coming through for me. I, then raced upstairs to my room, and quickly changed into something more suitable for travel. It didn't take long before mama and I were heading over to Trey's place, to borrow his typewriter.

During the drive, Mama and I felt a sense of relief, so, we prematurely celebrated winning this small, but great victory. When Mama pulled into Trey's driveway, I hopped out the car while it was still in motion. Before I could knock on the door, it suddenly flung open and there standing before me was a young man, that I couldn't identify. He was **about** 6 **feet tall**, with a **medium muscular build, weighing I guess at** about 175lbs. He was wearing only a pair of black Levi denim shorts and an enormous Kool-aide smile. He had a pair of deep dark brown eyes, which were fixated on me like I was a rediscovered treasure. Feeling rather uncomfortable, I mumbled Trey's name as I sternly stared back at the male figure annoyed because I was unsure whether or not it was truly my old friend.

The confusion on my face didn't go unnoticed because the young guy cleared his throat, then revealed his identity. He was Trey's cousin and his name was Scooter. Still smiling, he also declared he was very, very pleased to meet me. Humph! Once I was armed with this important bit of information, I immediately stormed pass dude and entered the house in search for my associate; he was in the shower. After hearing my voice, Trey shouted from the bathroom that he would be out shortly and told me to make myself at home. Once we were face to face, Trey apologized for his inconvenience before explaining to me that we had to search for the typewriter. Unfortunately, it was misplaced a week ago, when he painted his bedroom. "Okay!", I sighed reluctantly but Scooter announced he'd be glad to help me with the typewriter hunt, but wanted to know what he would get in return if he found it first? My reply was, "Anything". We straight way began our search for about 2 hours before we all agreed that finding the missing item was hopeless. I was in disbelief that I was going home empty handed. When my mind fell upon mama, I felt this rush of guilt because she was outside, sitting in the car during the entire visit. Oh my God! My mom was in the car, with no Ac, during a heatwave. Realizing this, I thanked Scooter for his help and bid Trey a short heartfelt goodbye, then exited the same way I came in. The ride back home was gloomy and quiet because my plan was a bust. Now Mama and I had to admit to ourselves that we were totally out of options on how to resolve our printing predicament.

It was now Sunday and the day was long and tedious as usual. Even though I was really tired from the day's activities of double church services, I couldn't fall asleep. So, despite my daddy's strict rule, I decided to sneak into the living room and watch some TV. I was stretched out on the carpet, quietly laughing at an old hilarious episode of the funny duo Abbott and Costello, when surprisingly the phone rang. I immediately glanced up at the grandfather clock in the opposite corner of the room to check the time; it was 11:30 pm. I wondered who could be calling this time of night? Was it a family emergency? Oh, my God, my mind was racing! After the second ring, I quickly picked up the receiver whispering "Hello" in hopes that my family wasn't awakened. I was appalled and peeved to hear the person on the other end of the line; it was Scooter. "Hello, may I speak to Anita?" he asked. I became a nervous wreck at this time because I was not allowed to have phone calls after 8:00pm from anybody, especially from a boy. I was momentarily dumbfounded and at a loss for words. To call a young lady's house this time of night was just plain inconsiderate and rude. Finding my voice again, I angrily asked through clinched teeth how he got my digits? He said that Trey's mom, Ms. Ann, did him the favor. I took a deep breath and asked Scooter what was his reason for calling me? I can only guess he detected in my tone, I was not pleased with his actions. Before responding to my question, he apologize first for being so disrespectful and inconsiderate, with his timing on phoning me. He sweetly conveyed that his government name was Charles Duke and he'd like to get to know me better. Since no one else in the house was awaken by his call, I slowly exhaled and took my anger down a notch and decided we could converse, what could it hurt?

During our conversation, we asked each other a hundred questions, only to learn we had everything in common. When I told him the date of my birth, there was this shocking shrill in his voice that nearly scared me to death. *Jeez!* it was like the second coming of Christ on the other end of the phone! According to him, we apparently had been born on the same day. Now I believed a lot of things, but this dude was flirting just a little bit too hard. I told him our conversation was over because I was not amused by his lying. Charles became irate and swore he was telling the truth. I placed my hand over my mouth and replied with a muffled voice, "Whatever". He shouted back, "Alright then, I'll prove it to you! "What's your address?" After I gave it to him, he abruptly just hung up on me. Little did I know; this nut was on his way to my house. It was about twenty minutes or so later when he dialed me again, only this time it was from the payphone at the neighborhood community center: adjacent to my home. I wanted to kill this dude, for calling me back! Did he not realize how late it was, Damn! He boldly requested for me to come over and join him, so, he could prove his case. Hesitatingly, I told him, "I'd be over shortly, give me a few minutes to sneak out."

When we were face to face again, I decided that maybe I could like him. He jokingly asked me, if I was ready to get the shocking of a lifetime? I mockingly replied, "yeah if that's even possible", then he pulled his state Id from his wallet and handed it to me. To my surprise he was telling the truth, we were indeed born on the same day. I swear, if I were for sale, I could have been bought for a penny. We stood looking at each other in silence for what seemed like forever before we simultaneously broke out into laughter. He got off his bike and we walked over to and sat on the nearby swings to resume our initial conversation. At this time, I noticed Charles had a sweet disposition and a wild sense of humor: he was very charismatic and intelligent too. But there was something else this guy possessed that I couldn't quite put a finger on. For this reason, I kinda placed a "BE CAREFUL!!!!" warning sign in the back of my mind. After talking for about another hour or so, we bid each other farewell and parted ways to our designated beds.

After re-entering the house, I had barely reached the top of the stairs to my room before I heard my dad making his way to the bathroom. Instead of waiting for him to summon me to make his coffee and breakfast, I took a deep breath and lazily made my way back downstairs to the kitchen. After fixing daddy his eggs over easy and toast along with his cup of joe, I was almost done with my morning ritual. The last thing I had to do was give daddy his insulin shot, then he'd be off to work. As customary Monday-Friday Mr. Greg would always arrive at 4:30 am in front the house blowing his truck horn for my daddy to come out, so they could get to their job at the Budweiser Plant on time. Every once in a while, I had the pleasure of serving Mr. Greg a cup of my coffee, these were special mornings because he'd always happily reward me with $10. He swore I made the best coffee in all of Louisiana. This not only boost my ego but my dad's too. Now that my early morning was free again, I headed back up to my room, slipped into my old blue nightgown, hoping to catch a few

Zs; however, I didn't get a wink of sleep. I laid across the bed, staring up at the ceiling thinking about my crazy late-night/early-morning rendezvous. I couldn't believe all the things that had unfolded in my life, in a matter of hours. I thought about Charles and our plethora of coincidences over and over until I suddenly remembered; I didn't believe in coincidences!

TABOO

DURING MY CONVERSATION with Charles, I discovered we iron-ically lived almost identical lives. For starters we shared the same birthdays, and were born in the same hospital within minutes of one another. Our moms were: the same age at the time they gave birth to us, they were both the second born to their parents, they were daddy's girls and the two even shared the same zodiac sign, among other things.

He and I were both the eldest of the same number of siblings, but they were opposite: I had three sisters and two brothers; he had three brothers and two sisters. We were also being raised by step-dads who fathered our last siblings. How-ever I was no longer considered a bastard after my step-dad adopted me and my sibs following his mar-riage to my mama.

Charles and I felt the anguish of caring for our younger siblings while trying to enjoy being kids ourselves. Despite the many respon-sibilities we were charged with at home, we still manage to be honor roll and outgoing students during the school year.

We often socialized with some of the same acquaintances, but until now, just never crossed paths. Charles and I enjoyed listening to different genres of music, preferably very loudly. We even liked the same types of cars and sports. We weren't too particular about crowds and often-times more than not we wanted to be in the spotlight.

It was clear that the two of us were: pretty mature, over-burdened, passionate, curious, adventuresome and complicated individuals. It was sad for us to admit even to each other that during our childhood, we suffered some form of abuse, although we never allowed others to detect it.

We had a sense of pride about ourselves and knew what struggle was, despite the fact that our parents tried so hard to disguise it. We were good at pretending that life was always good. We mastered the art of artificial smiles and we melted most of our pain away through laughter.

Last but not least, Charles and I were caught completely off guard when we learned that my daddy and his grandfather were friends for over 40 years. Yep! His grandfather was non-other than Mr. Greg. Who would believe a naive church girl with a stern well-to-do/preacher father and a boy living in the projects would ever cross paths with almost synonymous lives? Were we being duped by God or the devil? I don't know, but I was destined to find out soon enough.

WHEN SUNDAY COMES

FOR ALMOST A month, Charles and I had consistent late- night phone calls, while my family slept. The nights I snuck out to meet him at the community center or the park down the block were even more exciting. When we were out under the starry sky, it was then that he talked of this imaginary planet called **Zondria**. He described **Zondria** as a planet, a place where he and I could escape the real world to embark on new and thrilling adventures. It was through these stories that I was able to recognize when he was in a vulnerable state. I did my best to connect to him by holding his hand and placing gentle kisses onto his face for the duration of our meetings. With each night we visited one another, I was beginning to brood when we had to depart. WOW! Without warning, I became aware that perhaps, I was catching feelings.

The second Friday of August proved to be another extremely hot and blistering day. I had decided around 12:00pm to sneak away from the house to meet Charles at the Ice cream parlor several blocks away. During this unauthorized outing, I had my sister Sheila with me and Charles was with his best friend Irving Knight. I thought it was a joke at first when I found out Irving last name was Knight, yes, it seemed that everything pertaining to Charles was an effortless surprise. In between laughing and eating my ice cream, I managed to inform my boyfriend how my Mama was working my last nerve. She was stressed out because we still didn't have all the money to tie up loose ends for the church celebration: which was now just two

Sundays away. He gave me a big squeeze and asked "how much we needed to make my headache go away? I told him $350, thinking nothing more of it, and just like that, we went back to enjoying the moment. My get-away didn't last long but I wasn't to upset about it because Charles and I had the night to look forward to.

It was mid-Saturday morning when I got an unexpected surprise. I was lying across my bed in deep thought, when I was disturbed by someone, shouting my name. It was my baby sister, Leila, informing me that I had a visitor at the front door. Before I could digest what she said, my mom, and my two sisters Joyce and Sheila, raced to the front of the house. When I reached the dining room, I was in shock to find Charles leaning up against one of the dining room chairs entertaining the women of my family with that familiar big ole Kool-Aide smile on his face. For a minute, I thought I was in the twilight zone. My little secret was looking awfully comfortable and sure of himself, like he'd known my family his whole life. It was safe to say my mama, or Sweet Ms. Jolene as Charles affectionately began to call her and my sisters, fell in love with him the moment they were officially introduced. They all were seduced by his charm too. How-ever my presence made Charles somewhat nervous as he began to stutter and explain the reasons to my momma for his bold and optimistic visit. The (1st) to give her the money she still desperately needed for the church and (2nd) if possible could he get a proper consent to spend a little time with me. After no thought, Mama agreed to his minor request with a stern stipulation: be back in two hours. During our walk to one of our two designated spots, I informed Charles that my brothers, John and Franklin Jr., were out with my dad, Franklin Sr., getting haircuts. Whew! I silently, Thanked GOD my daddy wasn't home.

We entered the park and sat on our favorite bench near this huge Oak tree. It was positioned perfectly in the back of the park for shade and privacy. While sitting here we observed the children playing, and the grown-ups enjoying their dogs. During this time, we chatted and laughed about family and other insignificant things. It wasn't long before our two hours had come and gone. When this realization was upon us, Charles looked at me with an odd and creepy stare that made the hairs on the back of my neck stand up. Then, suddenly without notice, he gave me a peck on the cheek and a hug that seemed to last a lifetime. While strolling back to the house, I felt a strange sense of confusion and fear. When I was back indoors, I didn't say a word to anyone, I just went straight upstairs to my room: I fell to my knees and prayed. For reasons unknown, I urgently needed Jesus.

Charles was now allowed to visit me at home since his official introduction to my family almost two weeks ago. He had won my mama over easily but my daddy was not pleased or impressed. As a matter of fact, he hated the thought of Charles and I even being friends, let alone a couple. Every chance daddy got he reminded my mama that Charles was no good for me in every way but his words were like a room of steam, it filled the air but only for a second. In the meanwhile, Charles was bringing a different type of energy into our lives in new and unusual ways. He gave us our first initial introduction to a wicked device called "The Atari". This was a console video game that connected to the back of the TV. This strange and odd little black box had my family spellbound and hooked! They played this game into the late hours of the night, putting a pause to my late-night creeps out to the community center or park. Their second obsession with Charles was his clever way of making instant donuts out of regular can biscuits. He made these treats of his more appetizing and delicious by using different food coloring and confectionery sugar for icing. I don't know where he learned this trick from but my family treated him like he was the Pillsbury doughboy. The third and last thing he interjected into our lives was the card game known simply as UNO. Yes, these three little bitty things had my family eating out the palm of his hand. It appeared that Charles had become the surrogate king of our castle when my daddy wasn't around. That Be Careful Warning! sign that I placed in the back of my mind slowly began to move forward but I stubbornly refused to acknowledge it.

The day had finally come for the church's celebration. It was definitely a day that featured a list of *"guess what's."* We were mid-way through the Sunday school celebration when Charles walked through the church doors looking quite dapper but out of place. Our eyes were deadlocked the moment he entered and took his seat on the nearest pew to the church entrance. I had no idea that he was going to be attending the church service today. There I was, standing in the front row of the choir stand, looking like a deer caught in headlights. I was immediately snapped back into reality when the choir had to march around the church for the final offering. As I was making my way through the aisle pass Charles he casually slipped me $35.00 to put in the collection plate. I must admit, I was very impressed. I also was the envy of all the church girls within my age group ... and some older women, too.

The time finally arrived for the awards ceremony of the celebration, which some of us awaited with patience and assurance. My siblings and I won most of the trophies and awards because my daddy expected nothing less. But the element of surprise took me and Charles captive when mama lastly presented him with a trophy for the aid he administered to make the event an A-plus. The entire congregation rose up and gave him an awesome standing ovation as he advanced down the aisle to receive his reward. I felt like a proud bride watching her spouse receive the Key to the city. Once the awards portion of the ceremony was concluded, so was the church service. Moments later, I secretly learned from my sister Joyce that my parents gave Charles permission to bring me on my first official date. *I was delirious with anticipation as I hurried to the church bathroom to change out of my choir robe and to freshen up. When Charles stepfather Dallas arrived to pick us up, I bid my family a quick adios and we were on our way. Once inside the car, I exchanged casual salutations with Dallas and made funny faces with Charles three year old baby brother Dallas Jr..... I was anxious and didn't know where we were headed since the whole date was planned by my beau. I was eager and ready to enjoy this new experience. Today felt like a dream come true.*

Our first stop was the theater inside of the Gentilly Mall, here we were gonna catch the matinée of Superman II. We found very good seats and were busy chowing down on our popcorn and slurping our icees when a kid out of nowhere plopped in the seat directly in front of us. This annoying little person didn't waste any time telling us about the movie and its entirety. My first thought was where the hell were his parents? They owe us $22.50. Being infuriated and very disappointed, we sarcastically thanked the kid and left the theater. This jump started the second half of our date way sooner than Charles had anticipated, so we had to think of something else to do until Dallas arrival to retrieve us: so, we had to stroll the mini mall for 45 minutes. Before I knew it, I was being whisk away to Charles's home for the first time.

Charles and his family occupied a 4-bedroom apartment in the Langston housing project which was actually only a few minutes from the theater. As we traveled the short distance too the apartment, the nerves in my stomach began to become unsettled, I thought I was going to throw up. I'd never visited this area of the city before plus, I was clueless when it came to what to expect in or around any housing project; there was never any cause for me to visit one. At last when we pulled up to the front court yard, I was stunned that there wasn't much traffic or people outside, it was still the middle of the day. This calmed me a lot as I prepared myself to meet the Duke Clan. I stepped out the car and took a long deep breath, gathering my composure, I encouraged myself that as long as I be me, I'd be fine

Once I was actually inside Charles's home, my meeting with the family somehow felt nostalgic. I got to meet his mama, Ms. Lynn, his siblings: Larry 11, Michelle 9, Herman 8, and Sunshine 5, plus an uncle whose name I can't re-call. After the formalities of exchanging names, everybody went back into their rooms as quickly as they had come out. Although Charles's mother and I didn't have a whole lot of conversation, I didn't forget my manners to thank her for cooking some of my favorite foods, which by the way were a pleasant surprise and very delicious! I indulged in eating cabbage with rice, cornbread, potato salad, fried chicken wings and Blu-Bell butter pecan ice cream for dessert. This was indeed the major highlight of the date, so far.

Now that Charles and I were done eating, I didn't know what we were going to do next. After deciding not to wash the dishes we headed to the living room and sat on the sofa and listen to some Old R&B music on his stereo player. We were mid-way through the date when I was suddenly beginning to feel antsy. Being alone with Charles made me feel like I belonged to another universe, somewhere far-far away! We were enjoying ourselves with a fulfillment that I thought was satisfying, until he unbuttoned my blouse, while we were kissing but he didn't stop there. When the tune Choosey Lover by the Isley Brothers, started to play, that's when things became intense and the inevitable happened! I tried... we tried to have sexual intercourse for the first time! We were on the sofa making out one minute and the next thing I knew we had become half naked, trying to have sex. I was instantaneously jolted back to reality and knew that I was no longer in a state of euphoria! The pain I felt down below was cruel, horrid and unbearable. I immediately threw Charles off of me, which I found out later, proved to be a very bad idea. My hasty reaction didn't take into consideration that the nipple of my left breast was in his mouth. My impulsive action caused his teeth to clamp down onto my delicate flesh almost causing my entire areola to become detached. This was a type of pain I couldn't imagine anybody ever wanting to feel on purpose.

Although the sexual act didn't last a full minute, it made me feel disconnected from everything I ever loved. It didn't come close to the stories that I overheard from the girls who bragged about it in the female locker room of the school gym. I knew Charles had to be displeased with the incident, too, but that was really beside the point. Our chance at complete intimacy had come and gone, and I was ready to leave his humble abode. Charles tried to settle me down to resume the date, but it was useless so, he and, Dallas, honored my request and drove me home. In a matter of minutes, I was home crying and soaking in a hot bubble bath. During this time, I wished I could forget the travesties that ended the beginning of a beautiful day, but with no such luck. The day's events replayed over and over in my mind like a bad dream. I wish it was as simple, as a bad dream. I truly abhorred the feeling of disappointing God, my parents, and ultimately myself. I prayed to GOD for forgiveness and asked him to help Charles acknowledge that our relationship was done because I consciously had decided to move on. Unfortunately, the Heavens didn't send Charles this memo right away; he turned my world upside down.

Since my sexual encounter with Charles, I felt like I had lost an important part of myself. Deep down inside I believed that my mistake with him somehow tainted the perception of how I viewed life. This cause me to feel like an abandoned and trapped entity with no course or direction on where I was headed. I felt continual anguish as I searched for some form of comfort from GOD but there was none. Since the date, Charles relentlessly began calling and/ or trying to see me nonstop for days, but I stood my ground. I was not getting back into the bubble we had built around each other. He started to scare me and I didn't have the guts to tell him face to face that I didn't want to be bothered any more. It wasn't until we started the school year that my world seemed like a bad fairy-tale. Charles somehow thought it was a good idea that we should attend the same high school. This was absurd! He never went to his own classes, instead he just followed me to mine like he was my personal body guard. I knew I would never be able to breathe again until we had a conversation that was long overdue. With prayer and great persistence, I eventually convinced him to return to his old Alma mater. As the days came and went, his visits slowly cease but to my dismay, his house calls increase to a level that drove me damn near insane. Why was Life being so unkind to me?

I awoke last night to a very eerie dream filled with chaos and darkness: it involved Charles, me and our families. Three days later, on my fifteenth birthday that dream became a reality when Charles and I saw each other again. He came by the house to bring me a gift, which was a beautiful pen and lighter set. Although I was grateful for his thoughtfulness, I still had no desire to see him. It was evident only to me that everything about him had changed. When I was in his presence, I felt really unstable and panicky. When I looked into his eyes, I saw pure uncut desperation. This type of pain rarely ever goes away. I knew this type of emotion all too well, it was my sole reason for trying to engage in sex. After thanking him, I went back up to my room, thinking he would leave and return home but that wasn't the case. Instead, he remained outside for hours in front of the house pleading with me to come out so, we could discuss our relationship. Why was it so hard for him to understand there was no longer a relationship?

His visit took a real nasty turn when Ms. Lynn unexpected arrived at my residence. It was painstakingly obvious in her demeanor that she was not a happy camper, she was here **to** exact her motherly discipline upon her son. She walked up to Charles and slapped him hard across the face and tried to force him into the car with Dallas, but he made this difficult. He wiggled from her grasp like a wild man and took off running up and down the neutral ground. Dallas got out of the car and gave chase behind him, this only peeved Ms. Lynn off even more. During this crazy fiasco, my family made me know that they thought this was tragic and absolutely all my fault. They believed, I was evil to put Charles through such humiliation and I should be ashamed of myself. Their words and thoughts hurt me deeply. I knew they would never really understand the reasons for my behavior because of their love for him. How-ever, I truly believed after all the havoc and commotion it took for him to see me, on our fifteenth birthday, we were finally over. But fate wouldn't have it so!

MY FIRST LOVE

AFTER ABOUT TWO more months of agony, Charles finally terminated his quest of communicating with me. I was beginning to feel somewhat at ease and happy again. My attention was now re-focused on my studies in school and church. During the arrival of the cool and breezy days of November, I was devastated when things in my life spiraled out of control once more. I was feeling what I thought was the flu. My symptoms were: vomiting, loss of appetite and chronic fatigue. I decided that I should see a doctor, so, I made an emergency appointment with the health clinic for a check-up. My doctor's visit didn't go quite like I had expected it to. Lo and behold, I was embarrassed to find out that I was three months pregnant. I wanted to crawl into a hole and die. Choking back my tears, I remembered the countless nights I stayed up pleading to God asking forgiveness for the one and only time I fornicated with *him, who shall remain nameless*. I couldn't understand why I was destined to be back with Charles… with Charles *and* a baby! This news left me feeling very **scared and** really dazed. I didn't have any answers on what to do about this serious situation but I tried to convince myself that Charles didn't need to know. Who was I kidding? Of course, he should know! While riding the bus home from the clinic, my thoughts drifted back to the nights, I stayed up wanting to feel what my female peers called special: lovemaking with their boyfriends. I decided that this was something I needed to experience too, so, I let Charles in, never expecting a baby to be the end result.. ***I couldn't distinguish which was greater,*** *my baby, the blessing, or Charles, my punishment.* All I can say is be careful what you ask for, sometimes it comes with extra!

Being a pregnant teenager and a preacher's kid was a troubling anointing. *Thinking about how my family was being viewed by the church sent my emotions on a rollercoaster ride. It was hard to comprehend, that a few months ago, I was trying to escape from Charles but now he was imperative for me to thrive.* I found myself longing to go over to his house to feel better, despite knowing of Ms. Lynn disapproval of me. She outright denied that her son was the father of my unborn child. Even though this was hurtful, it didn't matter none, because her son never had any reasons to question my virtue. Without realizing it I began to really enjoy their family environment more than my own. The highlight of being a temporary part of the Duke family was the nights when we'd all clamor into Ms. Lynn's bedroom and watch a flick on something called a VCR player. This piece of machinery fascinated me, just as much as the cable boxes at my house mesmerized Charles. Our favorite movie was Lady Sing the Blues, starring Mr. Billie Dee Williams and Ms. Diana Ross. I liked being around Ms. Lynn during this time because Mr. Billie Dee Williams could put her in a mood that made you believe she was touched by an Angel. On the down side of things, I soon discovered that growing up in the housing projects was not so easy. There was a lot of violence, destruction and too many other grievances to list. *Despite the toxic environment surrounding us,* Charles, and I *still managed to have plenty of good times.* I got to view and slightly understand my baby's daddy from a whole new perspective. This made me long to love him the same way he loved me.

My guy and I embraced our adventurous nights, when he'd take me out riding on the handle bars of his bicycle. We went out scouring the near-by neighborhoods on the outskirts of the project, in search of electronics that people discarded with the trash. If we were lucky to find anything, Charles would bring it back home and work persistently to try and reverse its damage. I assumed this was how he learned to cope with his own personal frustrations and disappointments. Also on some of these nights, he tried to teach me how to ride a bike, but to no avail. Then, there were evenings, I refer to as special, when we'd just walk around the neighborhood and talk about the imaginary planet *Zondria, as if it really existed.* But these particular evenings weren't all about fantasies though; they also included us conversing about our real dreams for the future too. The direction we wanted to take for our profession was pretty interesting because we both wanted completely different things. Charles wanted to be an accountant or car salesman and I was torn between becoming a political scientist or an advertising executive. We made a pact never to stop dreaming, but eventually along the way we did just that. WE STOPPED DREAMING.

Despite being pregnant, I was determined to not allow anything to prevent me from getting an education. I enrolled into an alternative school only for pregnant girls. The curriculum seemed fairly basic and easy which was ideal for me. The school provided parenting class for its students and I was personally grateful for it...I thought our lunch would be much more healthier, since we were all with child/children, but the food was atrocious. For this reason, I especially looked forward to the end of the school day. I later on discovered that after school was dismissed, there happen to be certain teachers and students who, were enthralled with watching Charles and I. They found it to be romantic and cute when he showed up on his bike to ***personally escort me to the bus stop. He always made sure to bring me a drink and sandwich in hand***. These gestures were his way of caring for me, while making it obvious to everyone around that he was my man and my baby's father. It always amazed me how the little joys of your life seemed life great triumphs in the eyes of others.

It was three and a half months later when I dropped out of school because I had gained so much weight, I could hardly walk. This caused me great distress and put a damper on my joy. Going to all my doctor appointments stag was taking a toll on me too. I was overwhelmed and didn't have anyone that I could confide in concerning the emptiness that was swallowing me up whole. It's accurate to admit that when I was all alone, I felt terribly lost, depressed and miserable. I gave my hat off to Charles, who seemed to exude nothing but self-awareness and self-control. He had a perfect school attendance record and was a member of the JROTC club. He worked part-time at Burger King and with Mr. Greg in different parts of the city rehabbing his properties. For a fifteen years old teenager, he handled his responsibilities far better than some grown men, I knew. I believed he was going to be a great dad but as for me being a mom, the jury was still out. After waiting 40 weeks in suspense for the return of my body, the day finally arrived! It was on Monday, May 11, 1984, during my routine clinic appointment I found out I was indeed in labor; I had dilated 3 centimeters. After a brief examination and consultation, my physician sent me home with the instructions to walk as much as possible before returning to the hospital's maternity ward for labor and delivery. I tried to follow his orders down to the letter but I couldn't fight the notion something just wasn't right. Later that night, I was taken back to the hospital's maternity ward to await the delivery of my baby. After being on the ward for a couple of hours, I was given an ultra-sound to pin-point why I was having irregular labor pains and not dilating properly. It revealed my baby sitting upright in my womb. My physician inform me it was imminent, I have a Cesarean Section before my baby have an epiphany and stretch out its arms: which would undoubtedly kill me in the process. Yep! My little one is gonna be clever.

After I was prepped for surgery, I shared a brief visit with my momma. She told me not to be scared and that she was right outside praying for me. She notified me that Charles was outside in the waiting area also but was asleep on the floor. He made her solemnly promise that she would wake him soon as the baby was born. When they were ready to wheel me into surgery, mama kissed my forehead before she left my side. I was in surgery for two and a half hours before my son, Charles Franklin Riley, was born. It was May 12, 1984, at 2:15A.M. He was a big and beautiful healthy little boy, weighing a whopping 9lbs. 12ozs, and he was 23" long. My first son was now, My First Love!

Step into Motherhood

I am fourteen years old and just graduated junior high.
When on a mission for God, I met this guy
He swept me off my feet as we shared promises and dreams.
Things that were in our grasp, or so it all seemed.
We fancied one another, so we experimented with sex.
Not realizing that everything we do have a cause and effect
I was shocked to be carrying my very first child, but for you my darling
I'd walk a million miles.
I'm pregnant is this really true, the knowledge made me sad, but then I
thought of you
At fifteen, I'm walking about with a baby in my womb.
Never did I dream motherhood would greet me so soon.
I watched my belly swell right before my eyes, I'll always be your
mother, that cannot be denied
Carrying you was a task that made me check my faith.
My special bundle of joy you are growing at a fast pace.
I feel your kicks as you toss and turn inside of me, how wonderful and
special you have come to be
It's nine months later, and you want to be released.
Oh, how I wish the contractions would go away and cease.
I was ecstatic that time has come for us to meet, I promise to cherish
you from your head to your feet
The day has arrived, I get to see your face, A precious reminder you are
to me of GOD's AMAZING GRACE
I got my wish, you came into the world healthy and strong.
I never thought I could love so much, oh how I was wrong.
9lbs 12ozs you weighed and you were 22inches long,
You made my heart sing a brand-new happy song.
Welcome my son, into this cruel and vicious world.
Because of you I'm now a woman, no longer a little girl.
I promise to love you, care for you and to always be your guide.
A special place in my hearty you shall always occupy
You're my beautiful little boy, whatever more could I say? Thank you,
my prince, you brought me into Motherhood on this special day.
My First Born Son

It was four days later when I held my beautiful son in my arms because of something so awful and rare that happened to me. A couple of hours after I was taken out of recovery from surgery and placed on the ward, my sleep was abruptly disturbed. I was awaken by a nurse and a doctor, who proceeded to give me a vaginal exam and I didn't understand why? I tried to convince myself that I was in a state of disillusion, that this was really not happening. How-ever, the torture was so great, I honestly believed I was going to die. I must have passed out at some time or another because I had no recollection of getting back to my bed on the ward. Later that morning, I was awakened by one of the other mothers on the ward who was concerned about my well-being. Once I was fully coherent, she gave me the alarming info of what transpired with me. Apparently the doctor that examined me was not a real doctor but in fact a patient that escaped from the psychiatric ward. I wanted to sh*t myself when I heard this news. What the Hell! Sadly, even to this present day, I'm still dealing with the damage done to my body, resulting from this devastation.

My overall stay, in the hospital was a long and eventful six days. I went from being pitied to envied by the other moms who were coming and going on the maternity ward. Charles became my hero coming by every day to wash me up, aid in dressing me and combing my hair. He also played a vital role in helping me to sit up and walk again, I didn't have a clue it would be so strenuous to recover from a C-Section. I felt so lucky to have him in my corner as I noticed there were so many mothers, that were alone. On the other end, my family was totally in love with the baby, they didn't miss a day coming to the hospital to see him. He was one blessed and very loved big bundle of joy. The day we left the hospital for home, I walked into a huge family-filled baby shower. There was milk, pampers, and gifts piled up a mile high for my baby. He had so much stuff, the living room and dining area barely had enough room for us to maneuver around. Even though I was in great pain, I had a great time playing games and opening up all the baby's gifts. But I was tired out by the end of this special occasion. The day's most unforgettable moment came from Ms. Lynn. She didn't come bearing any baby gifts; she came only to perform her own personalized DNA test on my son. She boldly walked into my home, without speaking to anyone; not even Charles. My family and guests silently peered at her as she waltzed into my parents' bedroom and over to the baby in his cradle. With no hesitation or warning, she stripped CJ down from head–to-toe, then, wi***thout a word,*** she left just as she came in. After she was gone, my family continued to carry on, like nothing out of the ordinary took place. How-ever the drama over my baby didn't end there. Charles was in the den feeding his son when he overheard my Aunt Phyllis tell my mama that the baby showed a strong resemblance to my junior prom date from last year. Upon hearing this Charles became highly upset and mixed-up. This little/big incident got me so riled up, everybody that didn't live at my residence left in a hurry. Why would she say such a thing? My momma was the only person who could pacify Charles and ensure him that, he indeed was my baby's daddy. I was grateful that my momma had my back on this one, because all I wanted to do was go to war. The night ended with me and my baby snuggled up together falling asleep to the television.

Since the birth of the baby, my relationship with my child's father reversed to the days of old. He was coming to see me and the baby every day. We found ourselves laughing and crying as we reminisced about our good and bad times during my pregnancy. We both agreed we had a remarkable son who was blessed with a genuine love for music. What we couldn't decide on was who he inherited it from more, him or me. The biggest and only regrets I had about having my baby was the loss of Charles's grandmother and my great aunt Lucy weeks before he was born. They would have doted over my big chunk of love. For the moment, I was content with life!

On Mother's Day, I went to church with the baby and my family for the first time. My mama proudly showed off her grandson and I could swear some of the older female congregation were a little jealous of her genuine joy. I can tell you, there will always be some church folk who think very worldly and need to be watched. The last part of the service was the gift for the mother of the church. This year they decided to give out Mother's Day cakes. This was a first. I was utterly shocked when they called my name to receive a cake for the youngest mother of the church. As I walked up to receive this cake, I could hear the snickering going on around me. When I locked eyes with mama on my way back to my seat, I could see she was not happy about the stunt either. I winked my eye at her to let her know that everything was alright. There was no need for us to be irritated with mischievous church folk. Needless to say, later on that evening after dinner, my family and I enjoyed this cake with some delicious three flavored ice cream.

It was Sunday and Father's Day, and I didn't attend church because I wasn't feeling well. During his visit, Charles asked if he could bring the baby home with him since the day technically was about him, so I agreed. When my family made it home from church, pops wanted to see his grandson. When I told him that the baby was with his daddy, he became very upset demanding that we were going to fetch him right away. My arguments about Charles rights to his son were going on deaf ears with my parents, so, I angrily proceeded out of the house and into the backseat of the car. As we drove to the Duke's place, I stared blindly out the window wondering how Charles was going to react to my parents actions. All I could think about was how unfair all this was to him. When we arrived, I rushed out the automobile and walked over to Charles and interrupted his deep conversation with his neighbor. Upon receiving his undivided attention, I had to choke back tears as I tried to explain to him why I was there. He listened tentatively to me, but didn't get upset. Instead, he softly said he understood, then, he disappeared into the apartment and came back out with CJ and his belongings. Before I got back into the car, he kissed his son on the forehead and whispered in my ear, "Smile, don't be down, we have nothing but time".

WHO ARE YOU?

THE FIRST SEMESTER of my junior year of high school finally arrived. Charles and I had an extraordinary summer, but I wanted to put some space between us again. I knew that this was going to be a difficult task, especially since we shared an extraordinary new baby plus Charles fitted the bill for my school clothes and necessities. My desire was to get back deep into my studies, meet new people, and rekindle old friendships. I didn't know how to express this to him without coming off as ungrateful and rude because he had done so much for me, before and since the baby's birth. I soon had to digest that there weren't going to be any words that would make my separation from Charles a smooth transition. I attempted, repetitively, to **explain my essential desire for freedom and personal space,** but **he resisted hearing me. Just when I thought he'd gotten the hint, he showed up at the school with** baby, saying he was my husband, then check me out of school. I guess this was his way of expressing me he missed his family, but I was beginning to feel that familiar feeling again of being his possession instead of my own person. For example:

While I was tutoring an old classmate, who lived across the street from the school, one of his siblings informed me that someone wanted me outside; that someone was Charles. I became freaked out wondering how long had he been waiting out there. Trying not to show my agitation, I quickly cut my visit short and exited the house. When I caught sight of Charles, he motioned for us to sit on the school steps to talk. I put my best face forward in appearing strong, hoping he wouldn't see just how afraid I was. I tried every way I knew how to adamantly express to him my wish to keep our relationship cordial without unnecessary drama. When I finished talking, I knew he wasn't pleased with me because he walked away without saying anything. This left me feeling unsafe, paranoid and discombobulated. I felt like it didn't matter where I went or what I did, he'd be somewhere around hiding like a crazed stalker. Although it took a while to happen, Charles and I learned to co-exist without being as one for our son's sake. He eventually moved on to another female and I was reconnected with my old habits; along with the new responsibilities of a son.

The first official day of winter of 1984 arrived with a surprise. An acquaintance of mine introduced me to a friend of hers name Wallace Stern. He and I, became instant friends. I was smitten with him immediately and wanted more than a platonic relationship, but his heart belonged to someone else. Soon, I was visiting Wallace's home 3 or 4 times a week. It was always nice being around his 14 year old twin sisters, Trina and Tina, and his mother, Deidre. Since the first day I met them, they embraced both me and my son as part of their family. This made my friendship with Wallace even more special to me. Much to Wallace's unawareness, I was, indeed, falling in love with him. He gave me his undivided attention, as I frequently discussed the dilemmas I foreseen in my not so distant future. Afterwards he'd give me some good advice when applicable. He also swore that no matter what I ever went through, he'd have my back. His words gave me great confidence that I could really make my dreams come true.

During our winter break from school, I tried for a couple of days to notify Charles that CJ was out of formula, but I couldn't reach him, so I decided to pay him a visit. Before heading over to the Dukes' place, I asked Wallace to accompany me on my mission which turned out to be a very bad idea. When we were across the street from the apartment, I asked Wallace to wait there for me, I didn't need any unwanted problems with my baby's daddy. Moments later, I disappeared into the Dukes residence. Even though it had been quite a while since my last interaction with the family, they expressed nothing but love for me during my visit. Never-the-less, my trip appeared to be in vain because my child's father wasn't home. Of course, Ms. Lynn was all too thrilled to tell me that he was out with his new love interest. I thanked her for the information and was bidding the kids farewell, when Charles suddenly materialized. He walked into his mother's bedroom where we all were gathered, with a look in his eye that would have intimidated the strongest of men. Before I knew it, he angrily choke slammed me into the bedroom door. The doorknob sent a shockwave of pain to my back that had the intensity as though I shot by a double gauge shotgun. Hearing Ms. Lynn's demand for my release was voided to Charles, as he tighten his grip around my neck. He didn't let go of me until his mama clocked him over the head with her TV remote control. While standing over my slumped body, he explicitly explained his reason for assaulting me. This idiot said he felt disrespected that I brought *my man* with me to his home. At that moment, I really wished Wallace and I were indeed more than just friends. Gathering my wits, I boldly rose to my feet and silently exited the Duke's premises. I immediately knew it was going to take some strong praying for me to refrain from hating the most important man in my son's life. I managed to get within a few feet of Wallace before my suddenly collapse to the ground. He quickly came over and gathered my crumpled body into his arms and proceeded to carry me to his house; which was nine blocks away. I remained there until I was able to recover and make my hike back home.

On the slow journey towards my house, Wallace and I kept our conversation to a minimal. I knew he was relieved when we eventually reached my front door because he left expeditiously and without question. Once inside I retreated upstairs to my room, where I straddled across the bed wondering how could I block out the incident that burdened me in pure disbelief. I ultimately picked up my bible and tried to concentrate on reading scriptures to soothe my woes. I welcomed the interruption of the phone ringing because I had become more stress than comforted by the words of God: I was sure my

Master had grown tired of me. Hearing Wallace's voice on the other end of the receiver didn't seem to make me feel any better either. My mind was a thousand miles away as he repeatedly asked me about the baby's formula? After returning back to my phone- conversation, I let him know that Charles had just delivered it to the house, prior to our arrival. I wanted to address how upset and diminished the incident with Charles made me feel, but my pride wouldn't let me. To break the awkward silence that had imprisoned our call once more, Wallace suggested that I try and get some sleep and regroup in the morning. I tried to follow his advice, but this time I couldn't.

It became apparent and very clear, that, after all the years Charles spent hating his step-father's abusive behavior, it secretly harvested inside of him. As soon as I realized that my instincts about Charles insecurities being relevant to my safety were now justified, I became even more discouraged. Without notice this changed my feelings for him from respect to rage and then ultimately to disgust. With no notice or explanation, I made my mama the correspondent between the two of us, regarding our son. I expected this to infuriate him but I frankly couldn't care-less. After what he did to me, he was lucky he was not in a jail cell. I believed my frustration with him would slowly improve because he was now my mama's problem and this kinda made me feel just a lil bit better.

The last Tuesday of February of 1985 was Mardi Gras, it started off as a stupendous day, I never thought it would almost end with me asking God, "Why Have You forsaken Me? I had the pleasure of spending almost the entire day with Wallace, his family and my son. During the parades my baby was excited and scared of the floats and marching bands as they passed by. To reassure him that he was safe, Wallace brought him up to the floats to receive stuff animals and other trinkets. In conclusion we all thoroughly enjoyed the parades, food, the tourists and city natives who were out celebrating Fat Tuesday. As the evening worn on, I decided that the time had come for me to part ways and bring my son home. My friends thought it was a good idea for them to leave the festivities for their home as well. I exchanged hugs and good-byes with the twins and Ms. Deidre and went our separate ways. Wallace being a real gentleman was concerned about the safety and welfare of me and my baby, decided to walk us home. While walking along the riverfront in en-route to my place, Wallace ran into his cousin, Jeremy. Before I could blink my personal escort quickly excused himself from my presence and disappeared with his relative straightway into the darkness, behind the near-by buildings. Realizing that it was getting late, I was becoming increasingly anxious to make it home, my child had become extremely irritable. Just when I was about to forget Wallace and make my way home alone, he suddenly re-appeared and our stroll resumed, as if we were never detoured.

During our trek, we casually shared our thoughts on how we were going to end the night. My plans were to put my baby to bed, take a warm bath and read a novel that I had been anxiously wanting to read. He in-turn was going to try and reconnect with his girlfriend Lola. He was hoping to finesse her into letting him be in her arms, before the holiday was over. When we reached my front door, I kissed him on the cheek, thanked him, and wished him good luck on his quest before heading inside with CJ.

About an hour later, I received a frantic phone-call from Trina saying that Wallace had become mysteriously ill and they needed my assistance. I hung up the phone and hastily was off to see about my friend since my son was now off in slumber-land. After all, he was indeed my best friend and his well-being was very important to me. When I made it to the house, the family left in a hurry with the hopes of finding a drugstore that was still open to buy Wallace some medication for his: headache, fever, and chills. He and I alone knew the source of why his health had taken such a drastic decline. It stemmed from whatever it was that Jeremy and he smoked in the darkness prior to walking me home. Time was ticking by rather quickly and I was trying to wait patiently for Ms. Deidre and the twins to return but I had to get back to my own son. Meanwhile, I was trying to make Wallace as comfortable as possible before my departure, so I asked him what he needed? All he wanted was a glass of water. While I was heading to the kitchen, I heard him get up and run into the bathroom. I instantly aborted my assigned task and raced to the bathroom door to check on him. After overhearing him throw-up, I tapped on the closed door and asked if he was OK? That's when the unthinkable occurred!

I was totally unprepared for what the Devil had in stored for me. Wallace opened the door and snatched me into the bathroom. He brought me back to a place that I dared not to remember, for the keepsake of my sanity. I became acquainted with the bathroom in a sadistic and savage manner, as my best friend brutally beat and raped me. During this direful event, all I could think about was my CJ; he was the only reason I didn't want to perish. I lost all sense of time as Wallace did what he pleased to me. When he was done, he stumbled back to his bedroom, leaving me half-dressed and laying in a pool of blood. When I realized the attack was over, I painfully put my clothes back on and left his home.

When I left the Stern's house, I was defiled and wretched. I thought that Wallace and I had a friendship that would last a life time. I never thought in a million years that he would do something like this to me. While walking home alone, I soon remembered the one thing I abhorred about Mardi Gras. It was the emptiness in the streets until after the last parade has rolled. Little did I know, tonight this would become my Achilles Heel! During my long and quavering journey, I was unluckily attacked again. This time it was by a drunk that was full of liquid courage, provided by the festivities of Fat Tuesday. I could not believe this fright was happening to me; yet again. I was only minutes away from making it safely to my residence. Just as he was beginning to unclothe me from my already blood soaked garments, I found the strength to fight back. It appeared as though my assailant and I had been struggling for hours, before I could get the upper-hand over him. I managed to render him unconscious by hitting him in the head with the bottle of vodka he carried in a brown paper bag. *I was drained and just about defeated, when* miraculously, out of nowhere, a presence I couldn't describe or explain, materialized. It beckoned me to get up and run, so I did! Once inside the comfort of my bedroom, I shakenly went to my baby's bed and picked him up in my arms. I held him close to my heart, while I quietly wept.

The incident with Wallace left me broken and unable to return to school for a couple of weeks. When I was able to get back to the classrooms, I ran across him and knew right away it was crucial for me to transfer to another school. During **lunch time,** I ran into Eric, a very dear friend of mine, and confided all that had transpired between Wallace and me. His reaction blew me away because he promptly went in search of Wallace and found him in the bleachers of the school gym: he was hugged up with his new female love interest. Eric made his way up to Wallace and confronted him about his mischievous behavior, during our Mardi Gras break from school. Wallace, being pompous, snickered and responded with a smart mouth that everything, he heard **probably** was true, so what? It really hurt me deeply to know he felt no sense of remorse for the brutal and heinous beat-down that I suffered physically and psychologically by his hands. The brewing swarm of spectators *in attendance of this confrontation and myself included were in awe when* Eric *punched Wallace in the face.* The fight that ensued on my account lasted for quite some time because it was so difficult to pry the two of them apart, even after Wallace sustained a broken leg from them falling through the bleachers. Yet, the altercation still led to them both being suspended from school for three days. A vast majority of my female peers were angry with me because the fight ended Wallace's career as an All- American, so, fearing for my safety, I transferred to another school immediately.

The transition into my new high school went for better than I could have ever hope for under the circumstances. But I was feeling mixed emotions as I reconnected with some old and familiar faces, I hadn't seen since my elementary school days. It was laughable that I also ran into the first church boy I ever had a crush on too. There was a silver lining in changing schools that I hadn't expected though, I learned that my aunt/god-mother lived across the street: for me, this was a good thing. If I ever needed an emergency baby-sitter on a regular school day, I didn't have to worry because he would be only a hundred steps away. Yes, God is truly Sovereign. There was only one regret that I had about switching schools: it was the middle of 3rd quarter and I feared that I wouldn't do too well on my finals. However, I exceeded my own expectations and performed great, to say the least.

The start of the fourth semester was kind to me. I became friends with a girl named Theresa, who I thought was really cool. She had a 2-year-old daughter and we shared a common nemesis, some girl named Big Stank; she truly lived up to her nickname. I had no idea why this girl just didn't like me. She and Theresa were always at each other's throat for reasons I never quite understood, or cared enough to inquire about. Theresa became both a good and bad influence on me, but I was glad we were friends. Things were going well for a while as I took each day as it came with great stride and smiles. Everything was going well, until it wasn't. I just couldn't escape trauma or drama no matter how hard I tried.

The last month of school proved to be difficult as I became distant from everything that brought me satisfaction, once more. When I didn't get my period for May, I went to the doctor and got the news I was with child again. My mind couldn't absorb why this was happening to me, all over again? The strange thing about being pregnant this time, was that it didn't feel real to me. I felt like I was living someone else's life. But six months later, I'd soon realize it was my own. How could the doctors be ignorant of me being pregnant while I was hospitalized when having my tonsils removed in late March? It was hard to comprehend how a child managed to hang on to life inside me, after the ordeal I endured the night it was conceived.

I left the doctor's office and headed straight to Wallace's house. When I got there, no one was home, so, I left a note for him to call me later: which he did. At this time, I disclosed to him and his family that he was going to be a father. His reaction made me feel worthless and extremely depreciated. I couldn't believe that this guy, whom I once thought myself to be in love with, would turn on me like a vicious dog. He conveniently and convincingly denied ever touching me to his family, and I almost, I mean almost would have believed him too, if I wasn't the victim. Plus, he had the audacity to brag about the incident with some of my former classmates, with whom I still talked with, every so often. *A dagger went through my heart when he made the ridiculous* allegations that I was still screwing my baby daddy. Although Ms. Deidre didn't admit with words, she never doubted I was carrying her grand-baby. How-ever, child or no child, I knew that her going against her only son was not an option. I was deeply offended and filled with great affliction. I truly thought somewhere in Wallace heart that he would feel something for me and the baby but I was a fool. I knew deep down in my spirit that the things I was going through were just mere tests of my faith. With this in foresight, I knew that with Jesus, I'd conquer this situation which was thrust upon me whether I was ready or not. I was beginning to feel like a caged animal at home, so, I began to spend my days and nights at Theresa's place. While there I moaned and prayed daily to God for weeks that we move out of the neighborhood, where I spent the last ten years of my childhood. I truly loathed the thought of letting the neighbors, who thought so very highly of me, down again. GOD answered my prayers twenty-one days later, my family and I were moving to a different area of the city where no one knew my face or my name. I boo-hooed with happiness as I thanked Jesus endlessly for answering my small prayers. There was a point when I felt a twinge of guilt for not informing Charles of our relocation to a new residence but after reflecting on our last meeting, I quickly got over it. I had to admit to myself I was somewhat bitter. Still though, after the move, I was a bit overwhelmed and concerned on how I was going to fix the new and existing crisis which now plagued my life. Yes, I didn't have a clue on how I was going to survive and take care of my children, but I refused to indulge in self-pity. I was adamant and more determined than ever to remain focused and optimistic that everything was going to work itself out.

Summer came in again roaring with heat and craziness. I was basking in both freedom and disarray. I watched my siblings go from being innocent preacher kids to unapologetic rebels. They were feuding with the kids who were our new neighbors, for reasons unfounded. I thought it was hilarious how one minute they were arguing, ready to fight and then, with the blink of an eye, they were selflessly feeding their declared enemies. I guess if they wanted to have somebody to battle with, they had to be healthy. At odd times, I found myself wondering how my siblings were going to entertain themselves when we moved to our permanent home in the next few months. As I sat back being amused by my siblings, I don't think they fully understood how much I adored them. I often considered to myself if they thought that I failed them as a big sister. Even though my pregnancy had been an embarrassment to my parents, they were good grandparents. I found myself quietly smiling at the thought of how spoiled they had their grandson. As I marveled at the family's interaction with CJ, my mind would effortlessly drift to the new life growing inside of me. I hoped and prayed they would love and be as receptive to my new infant with as much enthusiasm as they did the present one.

Despite the rollercoaster of conflict, I was having with Wallace over our unborn child, my life was improving, until the sudden unexpected appearance of him! I had just slammed down the receiver ending another hair pulling argument with Wallace, when suddenly I heard a distinctive voice that made me cringe. I didn't want to believe it, but to my sorrows, it was Charles. I paused for several minutes before heading downstairs, I wanted to be reassured my mind wasn't playing tricks on me. When I heard his laughter again, I immediately became light headed. Slowly, I descended down the stairs and once reaching the last step, I sat down, feeling depleted. Here he was, beaming with exhilaration and pleasure while playfully throwing his son up in the air. The baby giggled nonstop as he enjoyed the reuniting with his dad. As I watched him doting over our son, I momentarily felt a stab of guilt for keeping them apart. When he turned his attention towards me, I became indignant because I hadn't forgotten about our last encounter. In a manner that was hostile and impolite, I asked him, "How the HELL did you find us?" He told me he simply paid my youngest aunt a visit and asked her where we moved? In an instant, I became wroth and livid. How dare she interfere with my life as if she knew what was best for me or my son. To contain myself I retreated to my room to watch television, as I waited for my unwanted guest to leave. After the uninvited visit from Charles, I became very discouraged. He was the last person on earth I wanted to see or think about. I was appalled that he didn't bother to give me an apology for what transpired the last time we saw each other. As if I could afford it, I now had another problem to deal with. It felt like my brain was on overload and I couldn't filter out what was good or bad anymore. I began to have long sleepless nights, severe loss of appetite, and a nagging desire to disappear, but there was nowhere to go.

It was almost a week later during my return bus ride home from my doctor's appointment, when I again heard that unwelcomed voice coming from behind me. Yup, it was Charles again, apparently, he was also headed to my residence. I was so distracted by the thoughts of the baby's heartbeat, I didn't see him when I sat down. As I turned around to face him, I was just too diminished to argue and fight, so I greeted him with a dull hello. He responded in a manner that surprised me, making the invisible barrier that stood between us non-existent. He got up and sat next to me, taking my hand in his, he asked "What can I do to help you?" For a moment, I couldn't speak. When I did, I asked him to just hold me and he obliged. I buried my head deep into his shoulders and we silently enjoyed the duration of the ride to my house. Once we made it to the house, we went straight upstairs to my room and I told Charles everything that happened with me and Wallace, resulting in me being four months pregnant. He collected me in his arms, and conveyed how much he missed and still loved me. He held my face up so I could look him in the eyes as he promised to take care of me and my unborn child. We made a promise to each other that no one would ever know that the baby that grew in my womb was not his and, just like that, Charles was in charge of my future again.

I moved back with Charles and his family on a more permanent basis this time. I was grateful and appreciative to Ms. Lynn for accepting me in her home, despite her personal feelings towards me. I came to understand that she had high hopes for her son and felt my existence in his life was nothing but a pure distraction and hindrance from him becoming successful. I imagined I would feel the same way about my son if he were in Charles's situation. I spent the greater parts of my days caring for my son, while trying to determine exactly what my role was in Charles's life. I was more than sure that the late-night phone calls and special visits he received while at work were from the same female he was dating during my absence. This ordeal with him went on for some uncertain amount of time. Finally, I had had enough. I informed Charles this was not what I signed up for and I was leaving. He apologized for the disrespect and said he heard my complaints loud and clear, then begged me not to leave him. Just like that the calls and visits stopped. I owed all this to Mr. Lance, a friend of Ms. Lynn and her boyfriend Dallas. If it wasn't for his company and advice I couldn't, or wouldn't have been able to survive my ordeal with Charles all over again. Because of him, Charles was now treating me well and Mr. Lance made me understand that I shouldn't have expected anything less. I viewed him as a long lost much needed uncle. I made up my mind that if I had another son, I would name him Lance Marshall Riley. One thing remained unclear to me, I didn't know whether to be happy or sad to have Charles to myself again. I soon realized my life was a hot mess.

It was on a cool and stormy night when the bliss that I was sharing with Charles was shattered. We were having fun playing and watching our son dance to the music on the radio, when all of a sudden, Charles became downright furious: CJ apparently soiled himself, instead of going potty. He snatched my baby off the floor and held him by one arm and proceeded to spank him with a force fit for a grown ass man. Because of this we ended up having a huge dispute which almost graduated to blows. I was not upset that he chastised the baby, but because his method and spanking was so harsh, my baby's bottom was severely tender and swollen. I had the inclination to leave for a while, but the unborn baby's weight on my pelvis made taking public transportation out of the question. I only had two options available to me, so I called my mama first to come get me and CJ, but she never showed up. Second, I decided to go over to Theresa's but I quickly remembered she had moved to a different address, unknown to me. Believe me when I convey to you that my meter was way pass full on disbelief, discomfort, discontentment, dysfunction, disquiet and dis-satisfaction. I tried to relax and calm myself down a bit because I was beginning to feel sharp and aggressive pain. For me, the night proved to be long as I tossed and turned, trying to sleep. I talked to my un-born infant, while rubbing my belly hoping this would soothe it, but it didn't work. By morning, my aches were intolerable, this caused me great concern and I began to panic. Through the midst of my pain, my heart leapt for joy when my mama arrived to bring me to my doctor's office. During my visit, it was discovered that I was in labor and my baby was breach, yet again: this baby had one foot in the birth canal. I was admitted to the hospital the next day for a scheduled C-section. These little ones of mine sure knew how to make an entrance into the universe. On November 25, 1985, my second son was born weighing 8.4 pounds and 20 inches long.

Who Are You?

How could this be? You stayed attached to me, through the beating
and the pain, you survived... it all, it's so insane
Who Are You?
When I learned you were there, it seemed no one else cared, but
that was OK it only reminded me to pray
Who Are You?
I felt alone and unwanted, the devil he laughed at me and taunted. I
had no idea of what to do, but I knew I loved you
Who Are You?
You came into my life so unexpected, the man that gave me you, we
were what he rejected, but God sent a miracle... everything is fine,
Mama will become better with the passing of time
Who Are You?
The time came when you were ready to arrive, whether I was ready
or not, you wouldn't be denied, one foot in the canal the other not,
a second C-section is what I got
Who Are You?
When I saw you later after hours had passed, the smile on my face
was no artificial mask, you were so handsome you resembled a
beautiful little girl, I was proud to be the mother who brought you
into the world
Who Are You?
You are my son, a delight to behold, someone to grow up strong
and bold
What the devil meant for my hurt, God turned into good. Never
have I regretted you, let it remain understood.
Who Are You?
My precious baby boy I shall love you always,
With every breath I breathe until my dying day
Who Are You?
YOU ARE MINE

My Second Born Son

He was so cute. As a matter of fact, most of the hospital staff and other moms that saw him, mistook him for a girl. It amazed me how something that started off so ruthless could turn around and become such a jovial experience. Later that evening as I lay asleep in my room, Charles arrived. When I opened my eyes, he seemed genuinely excited that I had awaken. The first thing he did was apologize that he wasn't able to be by myside for the surgery. I wasn't exactly sure how I felt about him being here after the disagreement we had the prior night concerning CJ, but after all the tenderness he showcased for me and the baby, I couldn't stay mad at him. I had to be honest with myself and admit that I didn't know where I would be if it wasn't for him. He exhibited genuine pride and joy when the nurse brought the baby into the room. As he held him, tears of joy flowed down his cheeks and that big Kool-aide smiled resurfaced. I couldn't even be offended when I learned he named the baby Chadrick Montrell Riley, without me. With this news, I made up my mind to call him Montrell since he wasn't named Marshall as I had planned. While watching him with the baby, I accepted that maybe he was always meant to be my knight in shining armor. So, bearing this in mind, I decided to give in and appreciate the fact that I had a man that loved me and my boys. I figured as long as our needs were being met, what I wanted was totally irrelevant. I made up my mind to not complain and to become the best mother and girlfriend I could be. I also vowed to myself, that I would try harder to love Charles the way he loved me.

The baby was almost a month old now and Charles and I had become equally restless because of his nonstop crying. We tried everything but just couldn't figure out why he cried so much. I knew something had to be wrong, so I took him to the ER. The doctor found a terrible rash under his neck due to extreme moisture left behind after his baths. The doctor concluded this was the source of my baby's discomfort. After receiving Chadrick's diagnosis, I was given two prescriptions for him: a skin ointment and children Tylenol. Then we were discharged home. The ER visit produced a false hope that everything would eventually improve and that our sleep would be re-established in the night again. My mama got wind of my sorrows and came by the apartment to check on me and her grandsons. After seeing the bags under my eyes, she felt sympathy for me. I was so grateful when she took the boys home with her. All I could think about was sleep, sleep, and more sleep. That's what I did for three whole days. When Chadrick returned back to us a few days later, nothing had changed for the better. His crying habits increased and he started to decline his bottle feedings, too. I was becoming dreadfully worried as any mother should be. I made a conscious decision that if things weren't any better over the weekend, I'd be returning to ER with my baby on Monday.

It was a horrible cold and rainy morning and Charles was running late for school, even though the baby had us up bright and early. The night before, Charles and I placed one of the two mattresses off the bed onto the floor, to alleviate as much movement as possible. We did this so, the baby would stay asleep when he did rest. It was about thirty or forty-five minutes after Charles was out the door that I had an unwelcomed guest. I awoke to Dallas being in our room, looking under the covers that were on top of me and my boys, because I was in bed, I was only wearing a T-shirt and panties. When he noticed that I was glaring up at him in shock and fear, he exited the room just as quietly as he entered. As the tears streamed down my face, it took all the self-control I could muster not to go to the kitchen and grab the biggest knife I could find and make mincemeat of him. Fearfulness and anger paralyzed me so much that Charles returned home from school 4 hours later and found me in the same position he left me in this morning. When he entered the room, he right away knew something was amiss. I was laying on the mattress, clutching the baby to my chest and weeping silently. After shaking me repeatedly for answers, the image on his face broke through the guardrail that shielded my escape from the violation of my privacy. I divulged to him what took place and within a matter of seconds, the Dukes' home was in an uproar. I was now crying frantically while trying to grab hold of Charles, as he broke into his mother's room in an effort to get to Dallas. My screams, his mother's yelling, and his siblings crying brought an unusual peacefullness over Charles as he released his grip of Dallas. He slowly backed away grabbing hold of me, while giving Dallas a stern warning of what not to do again, then we slowly walked backwards to our bedroom. When we settled onto the bed, he collapsed onto my lap and broke down in tears. To make matters worse, night fell and we had to endure yet another restless night because Chadrick continue to cry out.

Feeling ultimately defeated after vainly trying to console my infant, I finally caved in and returned to the ER late that night. I was elated that Charles had decided to accompany me this time with Chadrick aka Montrell, as I affectionately called him. My heart was reeking in dismay as I watched my little baby crying without a sound. I felt as helpless as the nurses and doctors who were unyielding in trying to find the cause of why my baby boy was in such an agonizing state. After an X-ray and a plethora of performed blood work, we finally found out what had been ailing my son. The test results revealed that Montrell had suffered several minor heart attacks because he was born with a cardiopulmonary heart disease known as Cardiomyopathy. Cardiomyopathy is when the heart is enlarged, but the veins that keep the blood flowing are too small. I was devastated. It took the doctors what seemed like hours to stabilize him, afterwards they transported him to the Pediatric ICU. I was afraid for my baby. I stayed with him all night, praying repeatedly to GOD for a miracle to make my son well. I begged him not to take my baby.

The following morning, pediatric cardiologist met with me promptly at 7:15am; he didn't want to alarm me when he informed me that my son had a rare blood type and would probably be in need of a blood transfusion real soon. He added that it would be helpful if I could get the baby's father family health history, if feasible. He said "this would be extremely helpful in treating my son especially since he was more than sure that Montrell's condition was more than likely genetically passed onto him. This little bit of additional information made things in my world a little more difficult to digest. In order for me to honor the doctor's request, I had to somehow get back in contact with Wallace again, without Charles knowing. I shuddered to think how Charles would respond if he was to ever find out that I had to embark on such a mission. I didn't know how, but I was going to do whatever it took to save my child. I convinced myself that what Charles didn't know, wouldn't hurt him.

Later on, that day when my mom came to sit with the baby, I went home to bathe, check on CJ and adversely visit the last known address I knew for Wallace Stern. My journey to Wallace's home wasn't a success because the Sterns no longer occupied the address that often frequented. The next morning when I returned to the hospital, I was reluctant to face the doctor. When I nervously informed Doctor Bryson of my failed discovery, he compassionately instructed me not to worry and promised that he was going to do his best to treat my son's illness. He advised me to keep praying because with GOD and time, he was going to help ease my son's pain and ultimately improve his condition. I nodded in agreement as I tried to remember that God was in control.

Taking care of CJ and tending to Montrell in the hospital was taking a large toll on me. I was no longer in school and my living situation made me feel restricted. I was a senior in high school with no hopes of graduating because no matter what, my kids came first. Although I spent most of my time at the hospital with Montrell, I did a lot of studying with the school books that I never returned back to my teachers. In total contrast, Charles went to school every day, and worked every evening. I was more than satisfied whenever he needed me to do his homework. It gave me some pleasure to pretend that the work I was doing was my own. It also gave me a sense of purpose when he got his report card because the good grades, he received were reflective of me. Still, I was in a constant brawl with my happiness and depression and nobody knew it.

The month of December was cold and wet. I had everything I needed for the babies, but I still needed some things. I especially needed a coat to help combat the cold, dreary weather. Charles was working with an old man named Peter, who made a living bringing trash to a designated dumping ground. Sometimes, they came across things that department stores threw away, although the items were perfectly new and useful. I remember like yesterday when Charles came home with about twenty to twenty- five coats, that were threw out by Gaylord's Department Store. We had no idea why the coats were so easily discarded. Charles demanded that I pick out what coats I wanted first and whatever was leftover would be distributed between our siblings and anybody else he could help. He always found a way to get us what we needed and for that I had so much gratitude and respect for him.

It was Mardi Gras of 1986 and Montrell was still in the hospital. After staying over all night with the baby, Charles and I decided to go home to get a little rest. While walking to the bus stop, we began arguing over something so trivial; I still don't remember what it was about. However, I do remember in the heat of the argument, I was crossing the street and got hit by a car. I was a mother of two who did not know how to cross the streets. Thirty minutes later, I was back at the hospital again, but as a patient. While in the ER, I became even more upset when the attending doctors and nurses had to cut off all my new apparel. But in the thick of all the chaos, I silently thanked God that I wasn't seriously hurt. After spending several hours in the ER, I was livid after my discharge from the hospital's care because I didn't have any damn clothes. I left the hospital in two of its gown and we headed for the bus top. Even as Charles stood alongside me, holding my hand, I still was very embarrassed as the riders on the bus whispered about my sordid attire. I felt like the butt of a very good joke, everyone was laughing but me. I was so glad when Charles and I made it to the apartment, I wanted to drop down and kiss the floor. The day's events left me quite exasperated, hungry and sleepy. So once inside our bedroom, my weary body plopped down onto the bed and instantly I fell asleep.

After being in the hospital for two months, my child's health started to show signs of improvement. He was now able to breathe without the help of the oxygen tube. I was so excited and grateful to God. I carefully picked up my little boy and cried HALLELUJAH!

LIFE OR DEATH

THINGS BECAME EVEN more interesting as the months passed. Just as things were beginning to get better for me and Charles, life began throwing more curveballs in our direction. First of all, Charles was graduating high school and had decided to make a career in the Navy Reserves. He chose to join the Navy because it had always been his grandmother's dream. I was unable to attend his ROTC Graduation Ceremony because I didn't have anyone to babysit the kids. Still I anticipated him going and taking me to the prom, but he never brought it up. After all the hard work I put in helping him pass his courses, I just naturally assumed he would bring me to the most important dance for all high school graduates. Needless to say, I was wrong. As I watched Charles walk across the stage to receive his high school diploma, there was a sadness that came over me that made it hard to breathe. Emotionally, I felt like the world was spinning and I was being tossed about in tornado winds. While sitting in the full dark arena, my eyes swelled with tears that felt like the size of hail. No one that was around me on a regular basis ever noticed the light that used to beam so bright inside me, wasn't shining anymore. After the ceremony was over, I continued to depreciate as Charles and a few of his classmates went about celebrating their success. I was left behind, not just because of the kids, but because Charles was beginning to get a taste of freedom and he welcomed it.

Secondly, I had to move back in with my parents for three months until Charles returned home from boot camp. Lord knows the last place I wanted to be was under my parent's roof again. Although it was turbulent at times, I had become really spoiled and accustomed to the stress-free environment, I had at the Dukes place. All I had to do was take care of my children. I didn't have to worry about being lectured by my daddy or feel like a misfit amongst my siblings. Being in the company of my family only reminded me of how much I fail them. Charles promised that once he got back we were going to branch out and get our own place. The anticipation of having my own house soon, made me anxious and excited for him to leave. Well, on the flip side of things, my family were jovial to have the kids back home with them.

The third thing that interrupted my life was an affliction, I wished I didn't have to endure again, so soon: Montrell was hospitalized. My poor son had pneumonia which caused him to have severe respiratory problems. The combination of these two ailments put a tremendous strain on my baby's heart. For me to sit and watch my son daily, with needles and tubes running in and out his body, was heart wrenching. I felt helpless, as I listened to the sounds of the machines that were in charge of keeping my son alive. My baby's weight loss displayed how fragile and weak he had become. He no longer appeared to be the healthy and plump seven month old infant, that belonged to me, instead, he resembled a premature newborn. His skin was so pale that you couldn't distinguish his race or ethnicity. The only two things that remained consistent and true to Montrell's features were his beautiful face, that made him look like an adorable female child and his with beautiful shiny cold black hair. The longer I sat and watched his swollen belly go up and down during his breathing, I began to felt so miserable and worthless. There was nothing I could do to change my little boy's situation. To those that saw me sitting with my son, I gave off the impression that I was strong but on the inside, I was screaming out for God to help my baby.

Charles left for the Navy the following week after Montrell's misfortune. It was hard for him to say goodbye to his son, especially with him being so ill. Ms. Lynn and I awoke early that morning to accompany him to the Navy base for his departure. While watching him check in with his soon to be superiors, I tried to keep a calm attitude and pretend everything was fine. I was determined not to display that I was breaking down on the inside. When it was time for him to board the shuttle bus that was transporting him to the airport, I couldn't uphold my strength any longer. Tears streamed down my face as I tried to make sense of the heaviness in my heart. All he could do was wave goodbyes with his hands and blow me kisses. I didn't know where to start looking for some form of reassurance that everything would be Ok. How-ever, the empty space inside of me became filled with uncertainty and depression. I unwillingly allowed, theses two emotions to take over my life and dominate my very existence. Uncertainty and depression became my two best friends.

Later on, that afternoon, while heading back to the hospital on the bus, I ran into Wallace and his estranged father on bus. It seemed like the day was going straight to hell. The sight of Wallace filled me with contempt and nausea, especially as I thought about all my son was going through. Wallace nervously approached me and cheerfully introduced me to his dad, before asking me "how I was doing and where was I headed?" Putting my personal feelings aside, I somberly sat between Wallace and his father and shared with them the calamity of my baby's health. Wallace father became outraged as he ripped Wallace a new asshole for not telling him that he was a granddaddy. He subsequently apologized for the both of them and wanted to know if I they could accompany me to the infirmary to see their offspring. I was relieved and overexcited with the offer as I thought about my son being able to finally get the blood transfusion he required. Depression and I were slowly parting ways.

Once we arrived at the hospital, Wallace and his father Gary were in awe of Montrell's family attributes. Right away, it was apparent that Gary could hardly stomach seeing Montrell's sickly condition. He walked over to the window to wipe away his onset of tears. Wallace was bewildered and beside himself with sorrow and pity as he urgently asked for my forgiveness and permission to play an active role in his son's life, starting at this moment. How could I say no? After Wallace and Mr. Gary gave blood for Montrell, they invited themselves to stay with the baby and me, all night long. I reluctantly began sharing with them all the anguish that I was feeling because I couldn't change the challenges that my child would face as he grew. They made promises of being around for the long haul but I had my doubts. It felt really strange that they wanted to be there for him, but honestly I was riddled with guilt when I thought about Charles and what he would think about all of this.

When the morning arrived, the three of us were worn out in regard to the baby's health and well-being. We prayed that the transfusion the baby received would alleviate many of his issues. After our meeting with the doctors, we went to eat breakfast at the diner located in front of the hospital. Feeling surprisingly jubilant and refreshed after hearing the good news about the baby, we enjoyed our breakfast with smiles. Gary expressed that he was glad to have met me and it was his honor to be a part of his grandson's journey back to good health. Shortly after we finished eating Wallace and Mr. Gary bid me a farewell. They both promised I'd see them later on that evening, but that never happened. In fact, Mr. Gary was shot and killed later that day during a botched robbery. As far as Wallace goes, I just never heard back from him, at all. I wasn't too keen or broken up about it because I didn't think it would benefit Montrell for Wallace to be in his life anyway. Looking on the bright side of our chance meeting, my baby's health improved dramatically. It's really amazing the difference one day could make. Both of my problems were solved and I didn't have to do anything. God is Sovereign!

A month had almost gone by before I received a call from Charles. He was so thrilled to tell me all about his training and how beautiful Sarasota, Florida was. He talked about the city as if it was the planet Zondria. I found it to be very exhilarating. After Charles finally settled down from talking about his experience, I broke down the details of my very boring, yet fulfilling life. I was more than delighted to update him on Montrell's improvements, and on how much of an energetic ball of life our first born was. We both agreed, our boys were our life-lines. As for me personally, the only thing that was different was my re-connection with Theresa, whom he hated passionately. We chatted on for about fifteen minutes more before he was off to chow and then bed. I wished him luck and told him how proud I was of him but I couldn't remember if I said, I love you before ending the call. After I hung up with Charles, my sister Shelia and I had a terrible and violent fight. This unnecessary action occurred because I didn't allow her to speak with Charles during our phone call. I couldn't imagine what she had to say to him that was so darn important. However, this isn't the reason why I became so enraged. In her so call state of being upset with me, she dared to compare my sick son to a dog. Needless to say, the brawl was very ugly and as always, I was considered the bad guy.

A few days later, I went to the doctor to see why I still had a period going on its six weeks. The news I got was disturbing and upsetting: I had suffered a miscarriage. In order for the doctor to stop the bleeding, I needed to have the same procedure that was done when women have abortions. I was baffled by this news. It completely diminished the joy that was trying to be in control of my tomorrows. After the procedure was completed, the nurse called my mother to come and scoop me up. Prior to her arriving it had begun to rain outside. As I **made my way to the car,** I was so shook up, I hadn't notice that I wasn't wearing any shoes. Once inside the car, the nonchalant attitude I had concerning my situation suddenly dissipated. I broke down into tears as I described to my mama the awful ordeal I'd just endured. All she could do was shake her head in what I figured was mere sympathy. Then we drove away.

I got a phone call from Charles again on Friday night, but before I could tell him what happened on Monday, he started to ramble on endlessly about how he would fail boot camp if he didn't dive into the water. I told him he was capable of doing anything and I demanded that he man up because we were depending on him. After he received the encouragement, he needed from me, our phone conversation was over. I was a little perturbed that I didn't get the chance to tell him about the miscarriage. I was struggling with the information the doctor shared with me about my reproduction system. I was informed that the odds of me conceiving again were slim to none and if I did, the baby wouldn't make it to full term or survive. I tried to make sense of it all as I jogged my brain on how this happened. Maybe I shouldn't have played football or basketball with the Duke boys and their friends, in the project courts after having a baby, only weeks earlier. Maybe it was due to the day Charles and I were riding bikes and I got thrown from mine after getting hit by a car a few months after CJ's birth. Or it could have stemmed from the second time I was hit by a car crossing the street in anger: months after Montrell's birth. Or just maybe it could be the result of the rough intercourse I endure from Charles in order to keep him happy. I took a deep sigh and decided to get my mind off my future problems by heading to the hospital to spend time with a child that I already had and who desperately needed me.

A month and a half had gone by, and Montrell was finally being released from the hospital. Theresa was coming by shortly to bring me to retrieve him. As I waited for Theresa to show up, the mailman brought me a huge surprise. I got a check from social security for my baby for a little over $12,000. I was super ecstatic to have two great blessings all at once. As I was Thanking God, Charles called with even more good news. He passed his diving test which meant he would be graduating from boot camp, and would finally be coming home. I knew time was overdue for me to return back to church, I couldn't wait to see the smile on my daddy's face. On Sunday we went to church. I sat with my kids in the pews, and it was obvious to everyone that my daddy was pleased. I was happy deep down inside knowing I made him proud.

Charles finally returned home and please believe me, he made an entrance. I was stoked to see him because his arrival was a complete shock to me. While we were greeting each other with hugs and kisses, my friends Rob and Darryl stop by the house. I had met the two of them one night when Shelia and I went out to one of the neighborhood bars for drinks. Since then, they had been coming over for the last couple of weeks to hang out with Shelia and I. Darryl decided to start sh*t, so referring to me he asked "Who is this man all hugged up with my girlfriend?" Of course, Charles went ballistic. Before Darryl could explain to Charles that he was merely joking, all hell broke loose. It took almost my entire family to get the situation under control. I told Darryl and Rob to leave before any more damage could be done to my personal relationship.

After everything had settled down, Charles and I headed out to dinner, he said there was something very important we needed to discuss. We managed to get to our favorite Chinese restaurant maybe an hour later. I was very nervous to hear what was on his mind. While we were waiting for our dessert, I almost fainted when Charles presented me with a black velvet ring box. He was proposing! I couldn't have phantom in my wildest dreams that he was really serious about spending the rest of his life with me. While sitting there looking at this beautiful ring, I didn't know whether to be happy, sad, confused or mad. When the waiter appeared, right on cue with a bottle of wine, I rushed around the table and gave him a delicious kiss and answered him with a simple and meaningful, Yes! The evening ended with Charles and me going to a motel, a sleazy motel for the first time. I was nervous about the lovemaking because it was going to be a painful event especially in lieu of the miscarriage I had two months ago. I did the best I could to pretend it was everything he wanted it to be. Charles relished in the fact that he took my virginity. As if possible, he became even more puffed up upon realizing that I had been faithful which was evident during the act of us consummating again. After sex was over, I headed to the bathroom and cried as he slept safe and sound. I don't think Charles ever realized the pain I endured when we had sex because of his massive oversized manhood. How was I going to bear this agony for the rest of my life, I didn't know?

Charles and I decided to rent and move into the opposite side of the duplex that my parents owned and occupied. The living room, two-bedroom, kitchen and bath plus the convenience of nearby family was perfect for my little family. Would you believe the night at the motel less than a month ago resulted with me becoming impregnated yet again? Upon learning this revelation, I was reminded of a childhood memory. I was six years old in first grade and my teacher name was Miss Stewart. She gave the class an assignment which was to draw what we desired to become when we reached adulthood. When she looked at my drawing, she was instantly perplexed. That night she called my parents to come in for a teacher/parent conference at the school. The next day, my mama and daddy came to see and speak with her about me as promised. Ms. Stewart expressed, how much she enjoyed me as a student and then, she got down to the nitty-gritty, my future goals. She went into her desk and pulled out and presented them with the picture I drew. The drawing was of me, a man, three boys, and a baby girl. My parents weren't the least bit alarmed. They did deem me to be crazy, and that was how they differentiated me from my siblings. Reflecting on that day, left me feeling dejected which caused tears to stream down my face without my knowledge. When CJ found me in the kitchen crying, he asked me "what was wrong?" I put on a cheerful face and told him that I was just so happy to have such a handsome big boy. I swooped him up in my arms and he smiled as he happily wiped the tears from my eyes.

MY LIGHT

MY UNEXPECTED PREGNANCY halted my education once again and I was forced to quit school. This time *I was not only dealing with Ms. Lynn denying another grandchild, but Charles denial too. However, the legitimacy claim of my child was the least of my woes.* Even though it didn't seem to matter to Charles, I never forgot about the stern warnings I received from the doctor that cared for me during my miscarriage. I made an appointment to see an OB specialist. During my visit with him, we spoke candidly about my past medical history. For the sake of me and the baby, Dr. Paulette strongly urged me to follow his strict diet with bed rest. It would have been nice to be able to follow his instructions, but being in bed all day was not a luxury, I could afford at the moment. I had to maintain a household, care for two small boys and a grown-ass man who acted like my third son. I knew it was going to be difficult, but I didn't have a choice. This was going to work out, somehow.

Since Charles returned from boot camp things between us were more than just trifling at times. One major issue was the ongoing tug of war between me and his mom. I didn't mind Charles doing anything for Ms. Lynn, but he had somehow forgotten, me and my kids came first. His mother had a man that provided for her and earned way more money than he did. Also, he couldn't treat us both like we were his wives. Besides, I could do things with and for him that his mother couldn't. Then, there were the countless days that he would spend all his free time with his childhood best friend, Irving Knight.

Yeah, Mr. Duke and Mr. Knight worked my last nerves with their late-night private drinking and partying. Things between us really became terrible when Charles began to neglect his responsibilities of taking care of the kids and household bills. I personally blamed Irving and the Navy for the stranger that was now occupying my bed. If this was what marriage would be like, I should pass!

I really should have followed the doctor's orders for bedrest; I soon came to regret my disobedience. It was a beautiful bright and sunny Saturday afternoon in March, when my families and I had an outing by the lakefront, which lasted well into night. While playing volley-ball earlier during the evening, I started having some strange discomfort but I brushed it aside as being normal pregnancy pains. Later that night, after we all made it home, I went next door to get Charles one of my mama's famous stuffed bell peppers and a small bowl of Gumbo. Suddenly, out of nowhere, a jaw dropping sharp pain, momentarily, brought me to my knees. After the pain subsided, I went back home and managed to put the kids to bed and tidy the house up a bit. When my chores were done, I took a bath, secured the house, and cut off all the lights. I was about to climb into bed when I felt this big plop fall from under my nightgown. I thought my water had broken, but I was mistaken! I didn't turn the lights back on to check and see what it was that fell out of me. In the dark, I promptly phoned next door for my mama. I know she was tired but it was painstaking for me, to know that she was not going to be getting any rest tonight. When she arrived at my front door to help me to the car, she painfully made me aware that I was bleeding very badly, and it was far from being normal. It was at that second that I started feeling strong and fierce contractions. I thought with all the confusion that was occurring, Charles would get up and come with me to the hospital, but he didn't. As a matter of fact, he carelessly shrugged off my situation by re-positioning himself in bed to sleep more comfortably. I was beginning to hate him.

I could tell my mama was getting worried as we pulled into the emergency entrance of the hospital, so I put on a brave face and be-gan repeating over and over to her that everything would be Fine....

The doctors assessed my condition as critical and straight away rushed me to the maternity ward for an emergency C-section. My water didn't break like I thought; instead, I was experiencing something called a *dry birth*. A dry birth is when the Placenta passes the baby, causing you to go into labor while bleeding profusely. I became very scared for the first time during my pregnancy. My baby was in deep distress and my blood pressure was through the roof. The last thing I remembered before I lost consciousness was the attending physician asking my mother "what sex I desired the baby to be? "A girl" she said. "I'm sorry, not this time." he replied, then with no warning I was out. While I appeared unconscious to the world, I was really asleep experiencing something purely Holy.

I was literally walking and conversing with God! It was outrageously magical. The fragrance of the air smelled like jasmine and sweet honey suckle. I was walking on a beautiful transparent crystal path lined with ruby and gold adorned lampposts. Above me were clouds that appeared so light and soft that it gave you the idea that it was floating cotton. During our stroll, God and I passed by angels of every race and nationality in golden robes who were once the relatives of the living. Their smiles were warm and welcoming like a cool breeze that you long to feel on an extremely hot and scorching day. The flowers I saw were the most beautiful bouquet of colors you could ever imagine. Oh yes, there was music playing, too. The sound of the angels singing praises to God was melodic. It soothed my heart and soul. For this cause, tears of joy poured from my eyes. The water from the running streams were an amazing clear hues of blue, it was truly breathtaking. God's voice was melodious and mesmerizing, His mere presence made me feel as though I was walking on air. There are no words to describe the emotions that overflowed through me as He and I conversated. I was in awe of the splendor and Glory that shrouded me; I didn't want to leave, but I had to.

I awoke, two days later, to find that I gave birth March 20, 1987 to another son whom Charles named Cory Irving Riley who weighed 6 pounds, 5 ounces and was only 10 inches long.

My Light

My first time in a motel was where
you were conceived
For the months that I carried you, your daddy didn't believe
I tried to attend high school with you growing on the inside, I
thought I could make it through it all. I guess I was a lie
Your daddy truly believed that you belonged to someone else
Never had I experienced such a betrayal to be felt
While carrying you, it was us against the world
You are more precious to me than diamonds, rubies and pearls
I didn't know if I would be birthing a male or female
But soon I would know what life for me would entail
My belly wasn't that big, I'm kidding…oh yes it was
My clothes were purchased extremely large for this particular cause
You flattered me by growing my hair and giving me glowing skin
I know I committed fornication, but loving you was no sin
You came into the world when you weren't at all ready
I did the best I could to take the pregnancy nice and steady
The after-birth shot right pass you, putting you in distress
Blood evidence everywhere, leaving a disastrous mess
I was rushed into surgery so they could save both our lives
It's funny how things went down, but we both survived
Finally, when I laid eyes on you, I was very distraught and sad
I wanted to give to you all the strength that I never had
But like a champ, my son, you eventually pulled through
I'm ever so grateful to God because he gave me you
You were so little and adorable everyone wanted to arm you
People from everywhere, some I hardly knew
You were a warrior to come back from the dead and live
My heart and life, to you, I promise to forever give
You did good and put up one hell of a fight
From the moment I saw you, you became my light
My Third Born Son

Because my son was born two and a half months premature, he was very sick. His lungs weren't fully developed and he had other problems that the doctors said weren't major, but were consistent with him being born too soon. During my only visit with him while we both were in the hospital, I fainted. When I saw how small and delicate my son was I became overwhelmed. He was in an incubator, under heated lamps, with tubes in his body running from almost everywhere. They were embedded in both his lungs, arms, and a shaved portion of the right side of his head. Before passing out, I did get a chance to speak with the attending nurse caring for my helpless infant. She stated things looked far worse than they actually were and to remain upbeat for him to have a swift and full recovery. She also said that my son's birth weight gave him an advantage most premature babies didn't have; that gave me great and little comfort. The fact that I couldn't hold my son made me feel somewhat void inside. I couldn't wait for his ill-fated despair to be over and for him to be in my arms. I wanted it to be more sooner than later.

I was discharged from the hospital long before the baby. My first day back home was the Saturday before Easter Sunday. My man and my family were all running around busily and I was a forgotten object. Charles left early Sunday morning with Irving to bring the boys over to his mom for the holiday and my family went to church as usual. Time flew by as I laid in bed helpless and asleep, until all of a sudden, I had difficulty breathing. I couldn't call out for help even if I wanted too, besides I was still home alone. While struggling and gasping for air, I managed to get out of bed and crawl into the kitchen. Because we were having a late spell of cold weather, the stove was being used as a heater to warm the house. Unknowingly to me it was giving off a large dose of carbon monoxide, nearly choking me to death. I somehow managed to cut the isles off before passing out on the floor. I laid there for an uncertain period of time before I could manage to get back to bed again.

Late into the evening, Charles returned home alone. He sat next to me on the bed and right away, began to apologize for his behavior during my pregnancy. He went on and confessed to me that he had been with the baby all day since dropping the boys off. He promised to make up for all the crap he and his mother put me through, then he shared with me how damaged he had become ever since the sudden death of his beloved grand-father, Mr. Greg last year. I had forgotten about the horrendous pain that the Duke family endured after the un-expected death of Mr. Greg. It was especially hard for Ms. Lynn and Charles to accept. My daddy took it hard too. Mr. Greg played a vital role in the caring for my first two sons. If it weren't for him, Charles and I would haven't made through some very difficult times. His un-timely demise came right around the time Charles believed he could show his grand-father his strengths: as a son, a father, and a man.

I remember how distant he had become and realized that noth-ing would ever soothe his pain, yet I remained hopeful that he would eventually be happy again. I also made myself believed that maybe in time, I and the kids would completely fill the gaping hole that was left in his heart. Upon gazing into his eyes I knew that would never occur. Charles broke my train of thought as he collected me into his arms and told me his family was the most important thing in his life and he was an idiot for not realizing it sooner. After everything he confessed, I never did get around to telling him about my ordeal while he was gone. I didn't want to make him feel worse than he already did, so I accepted his apologies and made a choice to move on. Was it pos-sible that we could really start over again? Only time would tell.

The following month Charles got a great job working at the Lace-Stein gas company with his Naval Lieutenant Jerry Bland. The money was really good, which seemed to make Charles more jovial and content nowadays. He had stopped drinking during the weekdays, spent more time with the kids, and began spoiling me all over again with flowers and gifts every pay period. There weren't any more com-plaints about household finances because he gave me the checkbook to pay the bills. On the weekends, Ms. Lynn got the kids which al-lowed me, Charles, and Irving too frequent the bar around the cor-ner to shoot pool. We also spent a lot of our Saturdays and Sundays listening to music and playing spades with my family. It's funny that we had cable TV, but never watched it. Charles and I were growing closer with each day. We were no longer fighting over trivial things; we were a team. I can honestly say that I was happy.

We were to endure another blistering and windless summer. The heat index was over 100 degrees almost every day. It was really hard to be comfortable at home because it was so difficult to cool the house. I went out and bought my sons a kiddie pool for their enjoyment and to keep them busy during the daytime. At night I allowed them to play in the tub until their little skin wrinkled. I was glad to know I had happy little boys who didn't require much to be satisfied. My sons made me feel special. The time of year arrived again for Charles to head off to Active Training School for the Naval Reserves. He'd be gone for a total of 12 weeks. It was difficult to watch him go this time around because the kids were getting older and smarter. They had also become accustomed to spending quality time with their daddy, particularly during the evening hours. Our only true consolation would be his phone-calls and the knowledge of knowing he'd be back real soon. It was about the second week of July when I received my first call from Charles; he had been gone for almost 6 weeks. He sounded so different and was very nonchalant during our phone interaction. I could tell something was on his mind, but he wouldn't divulge any information to me though. When I put the boys on the phone his voice changed to a pitch that was caring and endearing. I thought it was strange, or maybe I just was reading too much into things. I realized later on that night during the course of reading my novel, that he didn't tell me he loved me. Something just didn't feel right. Giving it no more thought, sometime during the wee hours of morning, I had finished my book and fell asleep.

Charles's called me two weeks prior to his return home from Active Training and asked me to come to Florida to marry him. He said everything was arranged and the only thing missing was me. Needless to say, I never made it to the airport. When he made it back home, we were to be married the following Saturday. The Friday before the wedding Charles and I did three things. We went and got our first driver's license, our marriage license and had a deep discussion about the journey we were about to embark upon. After several hours of weighing out our paths, we decided we should wait. All that was left to do was, inform my parents. We reluctantly went next door to my parents to inform them of our last-minute realization. My mama and daddy insisted that after two weeks of urgent preparations, a wedding was going to take place. They made me feel like I was obligated to get married because I was a preacher's daughter, who carelessly was having babies out of wedlock. And of course it was Charles duty to marry me; by all means it wasn't a choice, it was a demand. The day I got married was a fiasco and a sham from Hell!

August 1st, 1987 arrived, and I was a bride. My family busied themselves to make sure everything was in order, especially me. After all, they had been waiting on this day for nearly five years. I didn't like my wedding dress in the least bit. Charles and my momma picked it out the following weekend after he proposed. The dress was a southern style vintage dress. It had long sleeves and was made of satin and lace. I was required to wear a can-can slip to bring out the so call fullness and beauty of this monstrosity. My head piece was a vintage style wide brim hat that matched the gown to perfection and I hated it too. The attire failed to make me feel like a bride that longed to be with her King. My aunts dressed me and made me look as beautiful as ever, to their standards. After they dolled me up and took care of dressing themselves, the time finally arrived for us to depart for the church.

We couldn't afford to rent limos, so, Charles asked his Naval buddy Carl to be my chauffeur. I got to be first person to ride in his brand-new green Volvo sedan. Once I reached the temple where I was to exchange nuptials, the only thing that ran through my mind was the thought that this day was all a dream; a very horrible, horrible dream. I then, thought about how happy my mama was 10 years prior getting married at this same church. As I watched my four maids dressed in their light blue gowns march into the Chapel one by one to meet the groomsmen, a feeling of dread over shadowed me to the point of tears: I swiftly swiped them away. The people living across the street from the church mocked me by shouting two things my way as I waited for my cue to enter the cathedral. One person yelled, "you looked beautiful!" and the other shouted, "don't do it!" If only they knew, I didn't want to! I tried to pretend this was what I wanted, so I turned facing them with the biggest smile I could muster and told them that this was the day I always dreamed of, no way was I going to disappoint my one true Love. I asked God to forgive my fabrication as I turned, and walked up the steps into the building. I was destined to right the wrong I bestowed upon my family's name. As I marched up the aisle, I stared straight ahead, trying my hardest not to trip over my dress or my daddy's feet. My eyes slowly drifted to Charles standing there awaiting me in his naval dress blues uniform with a smile that gave me chills, but not in a good way. Once I made it to where I was meant to stand and exchange vows before God, my knees started shaking. I thought I would faint at any moment. The only laughable thing I could recall was Larry Duke, telling me to say No! when it was my turn to dedicate my all to his brother. Within minutes just like that I was now Mrs. Charles Antoine Duke. The guests gave us a thundering applause as we exited the church hand in hand. As we stood before family and friends taking pictures of us in front of the church, all I could think about was, this was never meant to be.

Once we made it to the reception hall, everything went to Hell in a hand basket! We weren't there twenty minutes, when Charles abruptly disappeared with no explanation. To add insult to injury, slowly my bridal party and most of my guest disappeared, too. After about an hour and a half later, I noticed through the doorway that the cars of my guest hadn't decreased, so I sat my boys down in the chairs on each side of me, before I got up and went outside to investigate what was really going on. My husband, my bridal party, some family members and guest were all across the street in the candy shop/pool hall, gambling and shooting pool. I just could not believe it! To say I was in HELL was an understatement.

I grabbed hold of the stop sign on the corner to steady myself as I tried to gather my senses. As I stood there, glaring at everyone in the shop that were meant to be celebrating with me on this day, I couldn't contain the tears that were stinging my eyes before dripping down my face. As I stood there staring at Charles and his crew, I felt my heart drop into the gutter. Was this a joke, it had to be? I couldn't understand why he even showed up to the church if he was truly against having the wedding. This was one of the most humiliating days I ever had to bear. I thought about all the sweet things Charles had ever done for me and I thought about the worst things I 've done.... After evaluating myself, I still couldn't determine why this was happening to me. I finally had gotten to the point of falling in love with Charles and this was how he repaid me. I wanted to retract my vows, my love and my respect for him but I couldn't. The most hurtful part of it all, he not only abandons me but he abandons our sons too. It's crazy, it's like he was celebrating his freedom not a marriage, how low is that? I didn't want to think anymore or feel either. All I wanted to do was go home with my babies, but I couldn't. Instead I was on a corner hugging a stop sign while crying endless. It seemed like forever before a friend of the family came to my defense. Feeling sorry for me, she marched across the street and gave everyone who shouldn't have been there a lashing of a lifetime. Within minutes of her departure back over to the reception hall, the wedding party and guest followed suit, but it was a little too late. Our allotted time to occupy the hall was almost up. It only took 5 minutes for Charles and me to cut into our beautiful wedding cake, which was a replica of the church where we were married and to thank everybody for coming out. I lastingly exchanged my wedding dress for a beautiful green and blue Jacquard suit. I kissed my boys goodbye, afterwards, into the green Volvo my husband and I went. Our destination was a complete surprise to me.

We drove up the street and around the corner to the projects where the Dukes resided. Charles wanted his mother to see him on his wedding day, despite the fact that she refused to attend our ceremony because she hated me. This was the moment I realized that grabbing the Champagne was the best decision I had made during this disaster of a day. I popped the top off one of the three bottles and took a huge swig before I was rushed onto the back of Dallas' 1967 pick-up truck; along with Charles and his siblings. His family and I traveled to the projects across town where Melissa, Ms. Lynn's only sister lived. I didn't understand anything about this day! It seemed that I had to see this nightmare to the end, but the end wasn't coming fast enough!

The next morning, I awoke at home with no memory of when or how I got here. I had a severe migraine headache and a desperate need to vomit. My head was pounding and my stomach hurt so bad I wanted to weep, but didn't have time to. I got up and staggered to the bathroom alongside Charles, in the hopes of reaching the toilet before he did. Sadly, at the same time, we both dropped to our knees and violently threw up all over the floor and bathtub. The contents of my stomach contained hot champagne and a tiny piece of wedding cake, but it looked like I spewed out a whole meal and then some. As if things couldn't get any worse, right after I was finally able to catch my breath and gather my thoughts, my menstrual cycle came down. The one thing I was sure of pertaining to the last 24 hours was that Charles and I hadn't consummated our vows. This was the only thing that gave me back some portion of my dignity and helped me gain a little of myself respect back. The thing I needed and wanted most was just a few feet away, so I cleaned myself up and afterwards climbed in bed next to my boys and slept.

AN ESTRANGED PRESENCE

SHORTLY AFTER THE wedding we moved into a new residence near Tulane University. In actual reality, this is the first house I could truly say was my own. It was a two-bedroom duplex, like my parents, and we lived next door to our landlords, Mr. And Mrs. Gates. They were a sweet and endearing old couple that genuinely wanted to help us along while enjoying our kids in the process. Mrs. Gates charms and her fat white bunny rabbits kept my boys happy, whenever I allowed them outside to play. This only happened when I did the laundry. We had been in our new home almost a week when I got my first guest and new tenant, Larry Duke. It seems that he needed me and Charles almost as much as we missed him. It was great to have a familiar face that cared about me as much as I cared about them. He went to school and helped around the house with no backlash, but he was a teenager, so, that required some form of freedom, of course. When he was away from home, I worried about him like he was my own child. My second visitor was their aunt, Ms. Melissa. Her one-time visit was more than comforting, it was welcomed and I'll always be grateful for it.

Charles was doing well on his job and came home tired and exhausted most days. I on the other hand was growing more attached to my boys, as if that were even possible. Ms. Lynn seemed to have given into the idea I was not going away so she made it her duty to let me know she truly missed spending time with her grandsons, so I re-instated her getting the boys every other weekend. On the weekends when they were with us, we took them to the movies on Saturdays and most Sundays went to church with my family. I wanted to do everything I could, so they would be well adjusted with both sides of their family. I began teaching my boys how to say grace before every meal and how to pray at bedtime. Once this was done, I'd tuck them in bed and read to them. I was destined to give my sons the knowledge to overcome any adversity. I wanted to teach them the value of self-worth starting now because I know they would retain all the information, I could teach them. Their brains were like sponges, it soaked up everything. I never wanted my sons to do to any woman the things I had to endure with Charles, for example, my wedding day. This was something I took great pride in as a mother. I was going to do my best to become an above average mom because I birthed above average kids.

Charles met a guy named Donald on the job and they instantly became friends. Charles and I would get together with Donald and his girlfriend Valerie, to play spades from time to time. On other occasions, we would travel about an hour out of town to visit with Charles naval buddy whose name was also Charles. I got along well with his wife, Lana. Hanging with the two of them made me forget about the woes of the city and everything that was wrong with my life. Lana and I saw life the same even though we lived completely differently. I had my three boys, while she and her Charles had just given birth to a daughter, whom they named Charlie Marie. For three days and two nights, our men ate properly and drank a combination of Jack Daniels whiskey and Coors Lights beer. Like good wives, Lana and I cooked and served them all day while we sipped on Bartle's and James wine coolers. The four of us would stay up all day and night discussing the problems of everyday life to laughing about common dumb sh*t. When our time together was up, we all hated to part ways, but real life was calling.

Out of nowhere, the comforts I had become accustomed to, were quickly disappearing. Charles was beginning to be away from home a lot with his promotion and new responsibilities at work. Although the pay raise was an enormous increase, I hated that my kids were missing their dad. When he was home, he was either to tired or drunk to spend time with them. It was my position that I was a wife with a live-in spouse that made me feel like I was alone and a single parent. Charles also started becoming careless with his naval duties. He had now missed his drills three months in a row. I thought that this was really stupid on his part, after all he worked for his Commanding Officer, Lieutenant Bland. I was clueless on what to do next. The most horrific thing about it all was the holidays were upon us. On Christmas Eve, Charles took me to the mall to shop for our Christmas outfits. I decided I wanted a black leather skirt with black leather boots and a white sweater for myself and I wanted to put my boys in black slacks, black shoes, and white sweaters to match mommy. I got them black hats, too. I consistently received nice compliments on the ways I dressed my little men, no matter where I went. This was a joy that even brought a speck of happiness to my mother-in-law's life also, especially when others admired her grandsons while in her presence. This was the one thing I think she liked about me. For me, one thing was enough.

As usual, things went awry while we were shopping. Charles and I got into a little spat about him flirting with the cashier of Dillard's department store. I hated making scenes in public so I wanted to end my shopping spree immediately. I headed for the car, but Charles didn't follow suit. As time passed by with me sitting in the vehicle, I became more and more infuriated with him. When he decided to grace me with his presence again, I didn't utter a word. I was somewhat happy though, because I had become hungry. On our drive back home, we stopped at a Checkers drive thru for burgers, fries, and of course banana milkshakes. We were pulling out when we encountered something that was never supposed to happen in our lifetime: a truck load of racists white guys. We were driving up the highway and stopped at the red light, and the truck stopped behind us, then, we heard one of the guys scream, "Get dem Niggers!" Charles and I looked at each other and I yelled "Go Bae! Go!" as loud as I could. He threw our 1979 Fiat standard into gear and shifted as fast as he could down the highway. That only encouraged the racist idiots to pursue us more. As fast as Charles could shift, the closer their pick-up truck zoomed in pursuit. They rammed us once and the driver of the pick-up almost lost control of his vehicle. Their initial goal was to run us into the canal that ran parallel to the highway. When it proved that this was not going to happen, the chase ceased and they bid us good-bye by throwing beer bottles and bricks at the back of our vehicle. Thank heavens all they broke was one tail light. After they disap-peared from our rear-view mirror, Charles and I took a much-needed deep breath in a sigh of relief. I don't think neither of us had ever been so scared in our lives. When we made it home, we both were physically exhausted yet relieved and absolutely grateful to be alive.

Charles and I awoke Christmas morning in great spirits. Mr. And Mrs. Gates were the first to wish us a Merry Christmas and presented the family with unexpected gifts. We were extremely grateful and Charles was even more relieved when he realized that I had bought the Gates a gift, too. After watching the exchange of the kids and the Gates opening of presents, it was proven that love was in the air. After enjoying the kids a few minutes more, the Gates were off to cel-ebrate Christmas with their own family. I was engaged in playing with the boys and their toys when Charles stooped down next to me and handed me a beautiful large red gift-wrapped box. "Merry Christmas, baby", he said in a tone so sweet and gentle that it brought a genu-ine smile to my face. When I opened the gift, I screeched so loud that it startled the two older boys and made Cory cry. Charles picked the baby up and insisted that I go and try my things on. He secretly bought my leather skirt, white sweater and black Liz Claiborne boots. I was ecstatic and couldn't wait to visit my family later that evening. That was one of the things that fascinated me about Charles, he could be a hopeless romantic sometimes. When he saw me, he was speech-less? It was so weird to have him drooling all over me in my outfit instead of him being excited about his own presents. It was almost like he was seeing me for the first time.

We had finally made it to my parents before we were to head around the corner to shoot a little pool, then take in a movie; at least that was the plan. The family were gathered in the dining room holding their sides laughing at some stupid joke Charles had just told them, when my sister Sheila walked in, interrupting our energy with her mere presence. Everyone turned around in her direction shouting, "Merry Christmas", and my mom asked her where she had been? Sheila replied, "Here, there, and everywhere." I told Charles it was time for us to head out. As I began to promptly bid everybody a good-night, something very disrespectful and disturbing occurred. Charles was still in his seat when suddenly, Sheila sat in his lap and asked if she could come with us? I was standing in the doorway between the outside porch and living room with a "what the f*ck" look on my face. Nobody found this to be strange and outrageous but me. How could this be? Sheila was seventeen years old and was a pretty and very well put together young woman but let's not forget, she was my sister. As she sat comfortable on Charles legs, he placed his arms around her and begin to wipe away her tears and said, "Not tonight baby". I slammed the gate to the porch and walked to the car hotter than fish grease. Of course, our plans no longer existed in my mind, but Charles being Charles refused to be denied. He went about the evening as if nothing happened. While displaying my anger, he had the audacity to tell me my behavior was juvenile and said this was one of the reasons he hated being around me. Instantly, I became mute. Once we were inside the bar, I sat in the back near the exit door and watched him and Irving shoot pool until they were tired out. Afterwards, Charles brought me home before he and Irving disappeared for the rest of the night to a destination, unknown. As I sat in my house alone, on my bed in the dark and quiet, I wondered why my life was so oppressed.

The year 1988 came in roaring. I thought Christmas was bad, but New Year's Day was worse. Charles arrived home drunk from attending a New Year's Eve party, asking about some damn Mrs. Fields cookies, which was one of his Christmas gifts. I sleepily told him they were on the kitchen counter and that there were only three left out the four because Montrell ate one. Then, I was abruptly woke up by the shattering screams of my two year old son. Charles felt he needed to be punished for this insignificant act. So this S.O.B decided to teach my baby a lesson by placing his little hands over the flames of the kitchen stove!

I snatched my son up into my arms, while cussing Charles out through a river of tears. I didn't know what to do afterwards. Pacing, I nervously ran down all the scenarios in my head of what could happen to me, my kids, Larry and even Charles b*tch ass if I called the police. None of it was good, the incident or scenarios. I began singing to my baby as I wrapped and bandaged his little hands. Oh God! I screamed out. What am I supposed to do? What should I have done? At this time, Charles regain some sense of decency and came to check on me and the boys. Seeing what he had done to Montrell's hands brought him out of his drunken stupor. He fell on his knees and started calling on God and all the Heavens asking for forgiveness. As I watched him, I wanted to throw up. The selfish bastard was only thinking of himself, and avoiding jail time. That's where he belonged but I couldn't do it. I was too terrified to call the police. I didn't want Charles to know I was more of a coward then he was so, I put on a brave face and told him to get the f*ck out. He hurriedly left without a fuss. I didn't know where he went nor did I care, I was just so grateful he was gone. The kids were sad and began to whine for him. They didn't understand why I was angry and made him leave, I just couldn't win for losing.

I didn't see or talk with anyone for the first two weeks of the New Year. I was sad and concerned about the state that my children and I were in. I felt helpless knowing that I couldn't protect them or myself. I prayed that my family would intervene if they knew what was happening in my life so with this thought in mind, I finally decided it was time to visit them. I still was having a difficult time processing what occurred on Christmas, but I figured this situation took precedence over my privacy. I told Charles I was not going to stay away from my family another day and I demanded him to bring me and the babies to see them. He looked at me like a madman, then yelled for Montrell to come to him. When the baby came, he sat him on his lap and unwrapped his bandages to check his burns. I guess he was satisfied with the progression of his healing, so he gave in to my demand. When we arrived by my parents, I was anxious and really nervous. As we were getting out of the car, my mama rushed over to assist with the kids. When she saw CJ her eyes got big as a full moon; it really showed how much she cared about and missed her grandson. She put three-year-old CJ down and went to grab Montrell's hand to help him out the vehicle when, he immediately burst into tears. She lifted him out the car and asked, "What in the world happened to this baby?"

I quickly answered, "Charles burned his hands over some Mrs. Fields macadamia cookies that he got for Christmas." "Yes indeed! "They going to put yall behinds underneath the jail!" she responded, before walking into the house. My daddy was sitting in his favorite spot on the porch at this time, apparently upset with what he just overheard. He didn't respond back to Charles who had spoken and passed by him. As I was going into the house behind my tyrant, my daddy grabbed me by the arm and said, "Don't worry! When you have your last snotty nose baby for him, he'll be gone". He let go of me and then said ever so casually, "Happy New Year".

Charles had been running around for almost seven months doing perfectly whatever he pleased, until the government caught up with him. After missing his sixth drill for Naval Reserves, the Navy sentenced my reckless husband to active duty. It was no secret that he wasn't happen with this decision, but he had no other choice but to comply. He was so distressed about it, I almost felt sorry for him. It was going to be interesting to see how everything with us was going to play out. The two weeks before Charles departure, was wild and crazy. He was running around like a chicken with its head cut off. He was in the streets most of the time and when he was home, he was either moping around crying or drunk. Even though we had money saved, we decided that the kids and I would move back in with my parents again. I was not ready for that. I couldn't rent the other side of the duplex next to them because they had recently acquired new tenants. One-night while I was packing, I began to develop feelings for Charles that only an enemy could understand. I had to dismiss the sudden urge I had to crawl into a corner and bang my head against the wall. How-ever, I accepted this was no time to have a pity party and dwell on regrets, I still was a mother of three special little men. My boys had aided me in horrific times with their unconditional love. Since their births, they made everything in my life bearable. To get through all this drama I had to remember that this, too, shall pass.

MY ADDICTION

THE DAY CHARLES left, was the day I felt a strong sense of abandon-
ment. I had no idea that it would be so difficult moving back home
again. Mentally I was truly tired and exasperated with the events that
surrounded me at this juncture in my life. I didn't know where to go
or what I could do for a peace of mind. But then, I remembered to
pray. A couple of days later, Theresa popped up at the house and I was
so happy to see her. We went to the bar around the corner and had
drinks, while reminiscing about old times. I enjoyed her company
so much that I asked my dad if she could spend the night. While
she was with me, I redeveloped a smile that was authentic and effortless. I didn't realize how much I missed and needed my friend.
The following week, Theresa called and said she needed to ask me a
favor. I told her to come by later that evening so we could discuss her
dilemma. Apparently, she was upset that her mom wouldn't take her
in, after learning her new residence wouldn't be available to move
into as promised. My friend needed somewhere to reside until her
apartment was ready. She and I were extremely glad and grateful that
my dad allowed her to stay with us until her situation was resolved.
I knew having her around me was going to be very entertaining, to
say the least, and I couldn't wait. We were together all of three days,
before I put her out. I considered what Theresa did to be a slap to my
face. It was inexcusable and heinous. She had sex with, John, my
fourteen-year-old brother. I felt like she violated my trust and puked
on our friendship. When she left my house, I was hurt and sad over

the incident because she was more like my sister than a friend. I knew I had to forgive her, but it was going to take some time. Man, the devil was really after me. I knew that I needed to get back to my relationship with God, but I didn't know how.

Charles called me the following weekend, of my falling out with Theresa, to tell me he would be coming home soon. "How?" I asked. "You just left?" He told me, he couldn't do Active duty. In order to come home, he was refusing training so he could be discharged from the military. I asked him "when he would return?" He said "he wasn't sure how the process worked". He promised he'd acquire his old job back and we would start all over again when he got back. I was at a loss for words. Wasn't there a limit to how many times we could start over? I didn't know. I hung up the phone in pure disbelief. One thing remained true, Charles was a coward to his heart and he could quit anything except me. I realized in his absence, I was a much happier person. Now that happiness would be strained with his untimely return and I wasn't sure if I was going to make it.

I was coming from my OB/GYN checkup, when I ran into Ms. Deidre on the bus. Imagine my surprise. It was just crazy that it was the same way I ran into her son. When she noticed me getting on the bus, she beckoned me to sit in the empty seat next to her. During the ride, she talked about the twins, Gary's death and Wallace of course. Finally, last but not least, she asked about her grandson. I took out my wallet and showed her his picture which brought her tears of joy. "Oh My God, he looks like Wally!" she exclaimed, while holding his picture to her chest. She then went on and asked if "I could bring Montrell to her home so they could spend time together?" I was not ready for the route this conversation had taken. She sensed my hesitation and began to plead, so my heart was compelled to say yes. I told her I'd bring him by on Friday evening, after his routine visit with his pediatric cardiologist. She became elated and beside herself with expectancy. Little did she know, I had two days to think over whether or not we were really going to show up at all. The day arrived and I found myself and my baby getting off the bus smack dab in front of Ms. Deidre's house. Her expression and greeting reflected that she knew I was contemplating on not coming, but here we were. She took the baby from my arms and planted kisses all over his face as she pranced into her home. I sure hoped this decision wouldn't come back and bite me in the butt. I convinced myself to take an even greater chance with my son's paternal grandmother by leaving him with her for the entire weekend. Need-less to say, I didn't sleep a wink while my son was absent from me. Ms. Deidre brought him home that Monday evening, before she went to work. She made the same promise as her son and the results ended up the same; I never heard from her again. It was a bittersweet reunion.

When my spouse made his way home almost three months later, we moved back in with his mom. The funds we had saved were gone because it took care of me and the kids in his absence. Charles didn't get paid salary during his time away. He was given a discharge, a DISHONORABLE discharge! He had the audacity to be upset when he couldn't get his job back working with Lieutenant Bland at the gas company like promised. The sole purpose of him ever getting that job in the first place was due to who he knew in the Navy. We filed a lawsuit against the gas company in the hopes of him getting some type of restitution and maybe his job back, too. I knew it was a long shot and a pipe dream, but I couldn't rain on his parade. So, for the moment, Charles was unemployed, we were back in the projects with his mother, while CJ was living with my parents and I was slowly but surely becoming unhinged. Dysfunction was now running around rampant and free and in charge of my little world.

The Duke household was in an upbeat frenzy as everyone were putting their best effort forward to ensure that Mother's Day would be chaos free the following day. Ms. Lynn was cooking some of my favorite foods, Charles was playing DJ, all the boys were playing together in their uncle's bedroom, and the Duke Sisters and I were busy cleaning up the place. The girls and I had started a game of tag and were enjoying themselves, so I thought. I had no idea what was coming for me until the last minute. I was on the bed, busy tickling

Sunshine when out of nowhere, Michelle came in and threw a couple of right punches against my cheeks. When I realized what had just happened, I was met with common sense that said not to retaliate. There standing in the doorway, was Michelle hiding behind Ms. Lynn with Charles standing next to her. He eyed me while sending me a subliminal message that if I cry, there would be consequences. What was I to do? As I sat there with all this anger flooding through me, I promised myself that revenge would one day be mines. Then God showed up and reminded me who I was.

After the incident and refusing to come out of the room, I naturally just fell asleep. Hearing my screams, Charles rushed in the bedroom beside me shaking me awake. I awoke in a bed of tears and with a river of terror rushing through me. Charles expressed genuine concern and showed a deep confusion as I tried to explain the reason behind my frightful state. When I finished getting out the last detail of my vision, we heard the loud cry of a woman making a tragic impact with the ground. The very thing I saw was unfolding at the exact same time I was explaining it to my mate. As the crowd gathered around the beaten and deceased woman thrown out her apartment window, I began rocking back and forth sobbing uncontrollably. Charles didn't know what to say or do with what he heard and then witnessed. Only one thing was clear, my spouse no longer viewed me the same.

Four months had passed and Charles was still out of work. That prompted me to apply for some government assistance from the state to help us take care of the kids. It had been almost 90 days and I still hadn't received any news yet. I was beginning to become uneasy. If things didn't get better soon, I was going to lose my mind. Charles adjusted to our environment by becoming a product of it. He decided to invest in selling drugs as a way of supporting us. It didn't last too long though; he was the poorest and saddest drug dealer you could or would possibly ever imagine. Upon realizing that street pharmaceuticals weren't his calling, he then decided to become an assistant shade tree mechanic to his close friend, Patrick. Patrick lived across the driveway and worked on cars behind our apartment. I swear

Charles knew next to nothing when it came to fixing cars. The income he generated from this charade of a job was barely enough to buy Cory pampers and baby wipes. *Hope* and I were new best friends, and I depended on her more than ever.

Michelle came home from the hospital with her son Samuel today. He was so cute. He gave me baby fever all over again. During the middle of the night, while everyone in the house were asleep, something came over me and I woke Charles up for the first time ever to make love to me. It was an experience that was not consistent with me avoiding or dreading the intimate act. The following morning when I awaken, I felt different, words can't explain it but it felt if though I had been born again. Over the next couple of months my habits and behavior began to change drastically. I became super clingy to my sons, I only wanted two things to eat, Yakamein and hot sausage sandwiches, I was extra sensitive and most of all, I wanted Charles around me practically all the time. I finally decided to confide in my husband that I might be pregnant. He frankly challenged the thought to the point of becoming belligerent and aggressive with me for even hinting at such a thing. It didn't matter whether he wanted to accept it or not, this was the only explanation in the world for my new and strange temperament. I thought he'd be happy, but instead he was beside himself with anger and denial. After I was going on and on about another baby, he decided that it would be best to have a pregnancy test before admitting me on the psychiatric ward of the state hospital. He felt this way because the doctors said I couldn't conceive again after birthing Cory. We went to the same clinic I had visited for my miscarriage to get a pregnancy test done. Surprise! I was definitely pregnant again. Charles was not supportive of me having another baby at all. He talked about abortion for the first time ever. I asked him was he crazy. I was having this baby with or without him. Besides, I just knew that I was carrying a girl. It didn't matter to Charles though; he was adamant he didn't want any more kids. He tried to talk me into drinking castor oil and when that didn't work, he tried rough housing with me to a level that was far beyond simple playing, but I never miscarried. I knew that carrying this baby to term was next to impossible and my life hanging in the balance wasn't an issue to me either. I wanted to have her because she was my miracle. She is what God showed me when I was comatose, after having Cory. For the time being, the both of us were at odds about this and in love at the same time.

Larry came by the project today in a black brand new 1988 Ford Thunderbird that instantly stole Charles heart. An acquaintance of Larry allowed him to drive it over the entire weekend while he was away on vacation. Charles was not satisfied until his brother let him get behind the wheel of this borrowed beauty. I had no idea that my spouse and this hunk of metal would cause me so much undisclosed grief. Despite Larry's plea for the return of the car, Charles and I were driving it around for about a week like we owned it. The day I urged Charles to bring the car back to his brother, was the day I became a felon. Charles and I were driving to my parents' house and arguing over his selfishness, when we were swarmed by police, only a few blocks away from the apartment. While we were being arrested and handcuffed for auto theft, Charles began to cry, asking the cops to let me go and not to hurt me because I was pregnant. His pleas went on deaf ears because we were both hauled off to the city jail. While we were being booked, the officers found it amusing to discover we were born on the same day. I was glad they didn't recognize that we also got our driver's license on the same day too. Charles and I weren't particularly interested in listening to their absurd theory that we met in the nursery and were meant to be together; at this juncture of our relationship, we considered it nothing, but a mere coincidence. I was *only* upset with Charles before the arrest. At this point, however, I was livid! What the hell else were we destined to do together as a first? My stay in jail lasted only a night, but it seemed like a lifetime. My cellmates gave me the 411 on what to expect when I got to court and everything they said would happen, happened accordingly. We went before the judge and for being first time offenders, we both were given 5 years of probation. Afterwards, we were released from jail on our own reconnaissance. When my momma arrived to bring us home, Charles shared with her the events that unfolded for us to become detained by the police. While they conversed, I was in deep thought about my children and my future. I then realized I needed to get far away from my husband as soon as possible.

While bathing and washing the stench of jail off my skin, I heard Ms. Lynn yelling for me to come get my mail; she obviously had no idea I was taking a bath. After getting out of the tub and dressing, I rushed to see why she had yelled my name so excitingly. When she gave me my mail, I jumped up and down crying, 'thank you Jesus' to the top of my lungs. I had 8 welfare assistant checks and 4 months' worth of food stamps. I immediately went to the corner store for a newspaper, so, I could search for my new home. My children and I were moved out of the projects two weeks later. I had true freedom at last!

I now lived across the canal, ten minutes away from my old residence by the Dukes. I was very pleased that I had moved in time for the beginning of the school year. This meant my boys didn't have to transfer from any other academy. On their first day of school, I was very blessed and thrilled to be walking with my babies. They looked like handsome little men in their uniforms. Walking back home from the institution was not as easy as it was getting to it. I began to have short, but severe abdominal pain and had to stop and rest for brief periods of time. Also, having a two-year-old didn't help my situation, either. I was ever so grateful that my landlord saw me suffering and gave us a lift home safely. I questioned myself whether I would be able to take care of this responsibility, 5 days a week. Charles wasn't available for us at the moment. He was still in the projects by his mother's place, trying to put a new motor in a 1981 station wagon for the benefit of us having transportation. He was also eager to be starting a new job in a couple of weeks as a clerk for a nearby Circle K gas station. Although he was needed here at home, I had no choice, but to respect his mind and accept that he'd be home when applicable.

After spending the last of our money, Charles finally got the wagon up and running. I was alone, as usual, after walking the boys to schools this morning when my part-time hubby showed up and offered to get me out of the house. He decided to bring me to see my mom and at the same token, bring Ms. Lynn to the meat market uptown near my parents' home. After leaving me with my folks and dropping his mom off at the market, I got some disturbing news about Charles. I was in the process of getting comfortable on the porch when I saw everybody in the neighborhood take off running around the corner. Due to my condition I couldn't investigate on my own, so I sent my sister Joyce in my place. Before she could make it to the end of the block, one of the kids approached me and informed me that Charles had an accident. As he was coming back to spend time with me, a guy in a stolen rental car, driving the wrong way, crashed into him. To keep from hitting civilians and other cars, he crashed into the porch of a nearby house, causing very minimal damage, which was nothing short of a pure miracle. After hearing this staggering news, I gathered all the strength I could muster to see for myself that he was OK and that no one else got hurt. When I saw only a glimpse of the wreckage, I felt lightheaded because it looked so awful. When Charles saw me, he immediately rushed to me and cried, as I held him. Even though he never said it, I knew he was grateful I was not in the car with him. His expression displayed how relieved he felt knowing that the baby and I were safe. This was the day that things began changing between us. Charles started to look forward to the birth of our new bundle of joy. I was so grateful and at ease that mama was able to retrieve Ms. Lynn from the market and return us all back to our awaiting homes safe and sound.

Once back inside my habitat, I was overly anxious to lay my eyes upon my sons again. When my mama returned from dropping them off at home from school, I was instantly all over my little fellows, overloading them with hugs and kisses. GOD, I love my babies! Later on, that evening after putting my kids to sleep, I laid in my bed in a fetal position rubbing my belly thinking about all the things that has happen in my life. The things that were no surprise to me because,

God gave me the gift of prophetic dreams. I can't, I mean I don't understand, why he chose to anoint a nothing like me with such a powerful gift. I didn't understand if this thing was a gift or a curse. I hoped someday I'd know. I began to giggle as I realized that God, Time and I were a funny threesome.

Since Charles started his new job, we barely saw him. When he was not at work, he was supposed to be hustling, whatever that meant. Our refrigerator broke down, spoiling all our meat, and we didn't have any money to replace it. If it wasn't for the pickle jar of change Larry gave me for the baby, my kids wouldn't have anything to eat. I was sending CJ whose 5 years old and Chadrick now 4 years old to the corner store with the change to buy $1.50 worth of lunch meat, a loaf of bread, $1.00 worth of cheese and 3 bags of chips for dinner on a daily basis. Just when I thought I couldn't take any more, my body began to feel pangs that scared me all the way to the moon. I secretly wished to hear the stories Charles told about our special place, Zondria. When the sharpest pain hit, I balled up, feeling like my baby and my body were infused in a horrible mess that wasn't supposed to be. And then Charles magically appeared. As I cried, he talked to my baby and the pains slowly subsided. "Don't hurt mommy, Don't hurt mommy, that's a good girl, Daddy's here" he repeated until the pain was gone and I quietly fell asleep.

When the next morning, I awoke feeling rested and re-energized as I literally rolled out of bed in search of my family: I found myself home alone. Charles left a note on the kitchen counter explaining where everyone had gone. He had taken the boys over to his mom's before heading to the job, which he would be working until midnight. After reading his message I headed to the bathroom to shower and incidentally almost stepped on Fluffy, the kids pet rabbit, so, I put her in the dresser drawer. I didn't feel like being alone, so I called mama to see if she could come by and get me. She was busy. I was regretfully disappointed as I hung up the phone wondering, what could I do with all this free time? I knew I definitely didn't want to be home alone. I came up with the idea to visit Charles on his job which was about a mile away. Yeah, this was a good idea, so I thought.

When I arrived at Charles place of employment, dude was genuinely shocked and confused to see me. In between his business with the gas-stop customers, we managed to converse about our circumstances, our boys and the new one on the way. I read in his eyes that he was really scared for us in these uncertain times. It's hard to disguise fear, and Charles had plenty of it. For the first time in a longtime, I wished I could give him reassurance that we were going to come out on-top but I couldn't and this made me a little sad, for him. When our casual conversation was traded-in for awkward silence, I took that as my cue to leave. Charles realizing that I would be walking back home alone became nervous and alarmed thinking about all the horrible things that could happen to me. I did my best to assure him I'd be fine, but he saw right through the lie. Therefore, he went against protocol and closed the gas station, until he returned from bringing me back home. He made me feel like I was important again and it felt really nice.

Charles had pulled off only minutes before I heard a faint knock at the door. To my surprise it was my boys, they had returned but to my dismay not to stay. Dallas brought them over to get a change of clothes because Michelle was bringing them to a fair. As I wobbled back to my room, the two older boys came to me upset, and belligerent, calling me a killer. I was stupefied and didn't have a clue why they would say such a thing to me. Right on cue as if they were reading my mind, they started to cry saying, I killed Fluffy! Oh My God, the rabbit! I forgot, I closed it in the drawer earlier. In this heat the poor thing must have suffocated. I felt so bad; I mean really bad! My little men were devastated as they ran outside to their awaiting paw-paw crying. For the first time ever, they left, without giving me a proper kiss goodbye but for the moment, I couldn't blame them. To my chagrin, it seemed that rabbit killer was now a part of my resume.

Within a of a couple of months everything in my life was out of control, yet again. I lost my house and had to move back on side of my parents duplex again. Charles no longer has a job. I didn't know the address where Chadrick's checks were being mailed to. My food-stamp card was missing, and I didn't have anything for my baby that was due in 6 weeks or less. There wasn't anyone one that I could turn to for a monetary loan or any type of assistance. I wished someone was available to give me some simple advice or just mere consolation. I was slowly losing my grip on reality. Oh, but what a difference a day makes!

I was waiting at the bus stop on my way home from the doctors today, when unexpectedly a young man still in high school approached me. Clearing his throat, "Excuse me," he began, "I don't mean to be disrespectful, Ma'am but you are the prettiest and sexiest pregnant woman I've ever seen, be blessed and have a nice day." Before I could respond, he was gone. I felt pure admiration for God because only him alone, knew I was feeling lost and invisible. Shortly afterwards, the bus arrived and I boarded and sat down in a seat, feeling like I just ate a piece of my great-granny's pound cake. After exiting the bus at my stop for home, I came to an abrupt halt, by Serena, a female neighbor. She asked me to come into her home to partake in a little conversation.

Once we were perched on the sofa in her living room, she right away began to confide that she's always admired me from a distance because of the animosity between her and my sister Shelia. She then asked, the sex of the baby. "A little girl," I announced all too happily. "I am so glad," Serena pleasantly replied. With a smile bright as the sun, she rose up and went to her bedroom to retrieve two extra-large garbage bags; they were for me. The bags contents consisted of clothes and other necessities for a baby girl. After viewing half of one of the bags contents, I hugged and thanked her, for what seemed like a million times before finally leaving her home. I didn't take the bags with me upon leaving because they were too heavy for me to carry. Therefore, later on that evening as promised she brought them to the house along with a baby bed and a stroller, too. I didn't think my day could get any better but it did; Charles got another job. He would be working for Stuarts Department Store and would be starting the following week. God truly saw my needs and met them!

The following week, during my check up, the doctor felt that I could be admitted into the hospital to have my C-section much earlier than anticipated. It was very overwhelming to hear that my baby was healthy enough to be born without any foreseen complications. This news was so unexpected, it felt like I had been suckered punched. I went home to tie up loose ends with my sons and make Charles aware of the doctor's decision but I couldn't find him for the moment. When I finally caught up with him, he didn't display any signs of relief. I was very disappointed in him and for the first time, worried for myself.

Later that evening, after being admitted onto the maternity ward for mothers undergoing induced labors and C-sections, I became a tad bit repressed. I thought for sure that I would have my baby's father undivided attention this go around. As I laid in my bed, I decided to stop focusing on my negative emotions, so I started to listen attentively to the other mothers as they shared their pregnancy experiences. One of the mothers lying in the bed next to mine began to divulge her bizarre and heartbreaking story. Her name was Tamika. She went to the doctor two days ago explaining to him that her baby was no longer moving. The doctor gave her an exam and, sure enough, her baby had died in her womb. She was admitted to induce her labor so she could deliver her still-born baby the natural way. After hearing this, I decided to go and take my shower. As the water ran down my belly, I began to shake my bump up and down to force her to move like she always do but this time it didn't work. I showered lazily and left out the bathroom, feeling panicky. I got in bed and balled up in a fetal position like always and pleaded for her to show me some sign that my mind wasn't getting the best of me. I needed her to move but she refused to until the wee hours of morning. When she kicked, I jumped up out of bed and danced, my happy dance. Oh, my God! I was so ecstatic and relieved. Afterwards, I laid back down, feeling more connected to my baby than ever. I was so amped that I would be seeing her face to face real soon, it was hard for me to contain myself. Time wasn't passing by fast enough.

When they finally did come and get me for surgery, it came as no surprise that Charles hadn't shown up to give me any support. This how-ever made me more determined, to make this C-section my last. While being prepped for I mentally promised myself that I would re-main wide awake during the entire procedure this time. I just had to see my baby girl when they pulled her out. As the doctors and nurses worked on me, they began conversing amongst themselves about how plump and stubborn my baby was being, then, suddenly, I heard this faint cry that lasted only a few seconds; she was finally here! When the nurse brought her over to me, she was beautiful. As she and I eyed each other, I made her a million promises. She smiled as if she understood my tears and I knew at that moment, my life would forever be changed because of her. **Next, I recalled the attending nurses becoming frantic, reciting my blood pressure was dropping, then I remembered nothing at all because I was out cold. On Dec 4, 1989, Charlita Jolene Duke graced the world weighing 7.14 pounds and 22 inches.**

My Addiction

I became addicted to you the moment I knew you were there, a
pearl you are to me, beautiful and rare
I was blessed to have had dreams of you before you graced the
earth, a treasure that came into the world who shall always know
her worth
I love your hair, your eyes, your little nose, the color of your skin,
there is so much I have to teach you where do I begin
You could never understand the joy you have created deep inside of
me; you have given me the courage to live happily and be free
I was scared of the world before you were born into my life, you
have assured me that I have the will to always stand and fight
I'm addicted to your laugh, your tears and the way you call my
name, now that I have you daughter my life is not the same
I 'm addicted because of you the moon, the stars, the ocean, the
trees and the sun that beams, Because God has given me you, I have
truly been redeemed
I can't wait to hear your stories that you shall one day tell, now I'm
destined for Heaven no longer living in Hell
They don't know me like you shall know in the distant future, I'm
free from all life's chains, you removed them away like sutures
A being that looks like me but will live a better life, to grow old in
Love, being a mother and a wife
I waited for you my addiction for twenty-one long years, Now I no
longer cry just sad and unhappy tears
I'll watch you grow into your very special self, promising to always
give you a love that'll forever be felt
I know you shall make the world a much better place, because my
little addiction you came to me by God's Amazing Grace
My addiction to you my precious one will never ever die, my addic-
tion because of you I have wings and I can fly
My addiction you will be the best version of me that all will be able
to see, Yes, my addiction I say you are the very best parts of me

My addiction you are the greatest that is yet to come, you are the
reason why I'm no longer living life so numb
I love you now and always from this important day, Mama will show
you more than words can ever say

My Beautiful Daughter

It was on the following evening when Charles eventually arrived. Although he was wearing clean clothes, I could smell the odor of oil and sweat on him from working on another car. He appeared eager to see the baby and stated he was proud of me, but never apologized for not being there when Charlita was born. When we made it to the parents' lounge, reality hit him that he indeed was the father of a special little girl. Lastly when our daughter appeared and they placed her in his arms, he became so overwhelmed that he couldn't contain himself from passing tears of joy. He installing kisses all over her tiny face and hands before feeding her. All the other mothers in attendance were admiring him with their plethora of oohs and ahhs, as he sang to her; it was so cute.

The fourth day after my delivery, the baby and I were allowed to go home. Charles and my mother showed up with the baby's things and both adamantly advised me upon my discharge to follow the doctor's orders. I thought to myself, yeah, yeah whatever, I just wanted to get home and cuddle up with my baby. Charles was so jovial as he dressed his little girl. She was adorned in: a beautiful satin and lace white dress, white stockings, a pair of white lace socks, white satin booties, a lovely white satin hat, a satin white bib, a pink snow suit and last but not least, an exquisite white satin and lace blanket. She looked absolutely glorious; we had our very own personal angel. When we were finally in the car, my mama wanted to bring the baby to see my grandma but Charles objected to that idea so we went straight home. Today was a very extraordinary day for so many reasons. It was snowing, which was a rare thing that happens in the south. For me, it was a reminder from God that my daughter was truly something very precious and unique.

SEVEN YEAR ITCH

CHARLES STARTED HIS job at the department store a couple of nights ago. It was a pity the store was closing in three weeks. On the last night of his employment there, Charles summoned my mama and me to come by after closing hours, to retrieve several bags full of useful merchandise that was thrown away by management. After we were done, my breadwinner went back inside the store, feeling dejected because he would be out of work, yet again after tonight. When mama and I went through our treasure trove, we were purely astonished by all the goodies we now owned. I laid claim to all the items that were befitting for my sisters and me, before disbursing the rest to the females we knew in the neighborhood. Everyone expressed their gratefulness to have new clothes that were for both the spring and summer months ahead. I know deep down inside that Charles was pleased with himself for what he accomplished in putting smiles on the faces of so many girls. I hoped this would give him some type of joy, even if it was only temporary.

I was so sorry Charles was out of work again. He was driving me stone crazy with his idleness. He left home almost every morning to put in a load of job applications but this still didn't suppress the funk he was in. I was completely baffled when his spirits abruptly picked up a couple of weeks later after making several visits to his mom's place. During this particular time Tanya, Charles's only female cousin and I had become really good friends. He and I both agreed that she was more than the perfect person to become our little girl's godmother. It was bananas to know that I had been dealing with her cousin for seven years and had missed out on having a close friendship with someone such as herself. It was cool though, we felt that we had all the time in the world to make up for lost time.

Things were changing. My household had grown and my family two-bedroom duplex was a little crowded now. Charles and I opted to move out and rent a bigger house from Joyce gentleman friend that was across the street and on the corner from where we now resided. Of course, something was destined to go wrong. I was truly grateful Ms. Lynn had come to get the boys for the weekend. This made moving into the new house less stressful. My baby girl and my new niece were asleep on the other side of the duplex with my family. We all were really perplexed when we received an unexpected visit from an estranged cousin of ours. I thought it was strange and peculiar that he didn't partake in helping me move, I thought this was the reason why he came by. Instead he kept himself occupied in the shadows of my parents' side of the duplex. At some point during his visit, he stole something from a young lady who lived across the back fence from my parents. Unknowingly to my relative, she was the girlfriend of one of the most psychotic persons that you'd ever meet. Here's where the crazy comes in.

While Charles, John, Leila, Joyce and I were busy clowning around and placing things in order inside the new house, chaos had started brewing at my parents place across the street. Shannon, one of our neighbors, had undoubtedly identified my cousin as the thief that stole a jacket that belonged to her best friend, Gloria. Her high and delirious boyfriend, Jimmy, and my guilty cousin got into a huge argument which led to a terrible and violent altercation. My cousin wasn't looking to good in the fight from my point of view. It was so brutal for my cousin, my mom and my sister Shelia got involved in trying to break the fight up. This led to a chain reaction of others in the large crowd that had assembled to get involve. Just when things couldn't become any stranger, I suddenly looked up and Charles was smack dead in the center of this heap of a mess and hit Jimmy with a punch, so, hard it broke up the brawl and the crowd. All I could do was stare down toward this monstrosity with a sh*t look on my face. Moments later, Charles comes to me shaken up and disturbed asking me "What have I done?" "What were you thinking?" I muttered. "I thought he hit Jolene," he whined before jumping into our car and speeding down the block out of sight. He was gone before I could fully process what the hell, he had just done.

Seconds later, my battered cousin walked up to me and I didn't waste time telling him that it was in his best interest to leave from around our parts because if he didn't, he was a dead man. Once he was gone, almost my entire family were now standing in my new living room looking nervous and stumped. With no regard for fear, I made up my mind to go and check on my daddy and the babies. My remaining love ones were more comfortable with sitting this mission out. I couldn't blame them though; I truly understood their apprehension, so, I didn't put up a fuss as they stayed behind.

As I approached the residence, I was angry that the front door was left wide open. Upon entering the house, I heard my poor father calling out for a drink of water. I had just taken care of his needs, made sure the babies were secured and was walking out of the dwelling when Jimmy re-appeared again. He aggressively brushed past me and entered the premises looking for my cousin, which only took him a minute to realize wasn't here. He found me standing a few feet from the house entrance and walked up to me, placing a nine milometer Glock against the center of my forehead and asked me in a voice that was low and sadistic, "Where is he?" "He's not here," I said. As we stood there eye to eye, I knew I was standing face to face with the world's interpretation of what the devil is supposed resemble, but I was not afraid. "Bitch, I..." was all he managed to get out through clinched teeth, before I heard Gloria shout, "Jimmy! No! Leave that girl alone!" At that moment, she met up with Jimmy and was side by side with him lowering the gun, while at the same time whispering to me, she was sorry. They walked away and I continued to travel on to my awaiting family to let them know that they were safe again. They were jovial to return home because everything was now back to normal. I resumed moving my things into the new place for the remainder of the night, up until the wee hours. After I was almost complete, Charles miraculously popped back up. He began to tell me about his disappearance, while I was preparing for bed. I calmly interrupted and advised him not to wake up Charlita because I just put her back to sleep. He had no idea I couldn't care-less about where he had gone to or his reason for leaving. All I knew was that he abandoned me plus our daughter, and I would never forget it.

A couple of months had passed when I noticed a difference with Tanya and John. I'm not exactly sure, how or when Tanya and my brother John hooked up and became a couple, but they became almost inseparable. The two were at my house visiting nearly every day or/and night. I must admit, Charles and I welcomed and enjoyed their company a great deal. They were a great distraction for the two of us because we didn't have to deal with each other. The first night they stayed over, we were all up until the crack of dawn playing cards and acting like plum fools as we joked and laughed at the stupidest things. It was a great time.

Later on, that morning, Charles left out scouring for employment again and my brother went home across the street to my parents' house. An hour later, Dallas and Ms. Lynn came by and retrieved their grandsons. Tanya took Charlita for the day, which left me home by myself. After the house was completely cleared out, I went outside and sat on the steps to feel a little sunshine. As I was sitting enjoying the weather, I was staring down the street towards my parents place when I noticed Shannon, our neighbor, and her boyfriend Robert arrive home with their new daughter. As Robert was about to exit their vehicle another car pulled up right beside them. Immediately, two guys jumped out, armed with shot guns were yelling and demanding something from him. I couldn't hear what they were asking for because I was so far away. Before I could grasp what was happening, I was instantly horrified as I witnessed Robert get shot by one of the two gunmen. Just as fast as they came, they were gone. I sat there and witnessed this travesty from beginning to end without being able to scream, talk or move. I duly noted that I was the only neighbor outside while all this was taking place. When I did get control of my extremities again, I slowly got up and went inside. I was convinced that what I just witnessed was the screen play of a very bad movie... until the police showed up. I kept what I saw to myself, for reasons unknown.

Charles getting up every morning had finally paid off; he got another job working at another gas station as a clerk. It was so hard for him to sleep because he was full of anxiety as he awaited his first day of employment. The only thing that gave him comfort was the idea of knowing that he would be working in a few days. I wasn't sure if he was going to make it.

My husband had been working steadily for three months and thought it was time for us to have a different scenery. On his next day off, we went house hunting and I found the house of my dreams. It was a two-story cottage style home with a private driveway and separate washing quarters. I was pleased with the realization that the school for the kids was only two blocks away and the supermarket was in walking distance. After surveying the house from the outside, we desperately wanted to see the inside of this beauty. When we arrived at the realty company, we were told they no longer needed to personally escort potential tenants for their properties. Instead, we had to put down a $50 key deposit to inspect the interior of the house. We left the company **heartbroken because it was** something, we didn't have for the moment.

Once we were in the car again, I tearfully instructed Charles to pass by the house one more time, so I could say farewell to it. While we were driving away from the property, I spotted a wallet in the middle of the street, so we pulled over to pick it up and checked it contents. Low and behold it was for a nearby resident who must have lost it while jogging. The wallet contained the exact amount of money we needed to see the inner part of the house. We put the wallet in the owner's mailbox and took the cash and went straight back to the realty company. Charles Duke, with his smooth talking butt, convinced the lady employee at the realty company to take the house off the market until he got paid the following weekend. This made me a happy woman! Sadly, my joy was a very short lived experience.

Tanya and I had grown really close and we considered each other sisters. When I saw her about to jeopardize her education for John, I couldn't idly standby and say nothing. After I gave her some sound advice, she took my words with a grain of salt and thanked me by returning the favor of trying to save my future by giving me information about my husband. Apparently, my spouse had been cheating on me with someone he met also serving in the military, when he was a member. It appeared this was something that my dear mother-in-law knew too. There were even pictures that could back up the allegations. With this truth being revealed, Tanya knew that she had put her relationship with her favorite cousin in jeopardy because of me and that hurt me greatly. Boy! I knew I was going to miss her. Just when I thought I couldn't stomach another heart wrenching disappointment from Charles, there came an even greater challenge to test the strength of my loyalty of being married to this jerk.

I was at my parents' home spending time with my daddy when I was approached by Shelia, Leila and their new best friend, Nooky. It seemed they had something that was necessary for me to know and it required immediate attention. They pulled me to the side and one by one preceded to spin me a tale of Charles touching them inappropriately. This was too much for my mind to digest. The only solace I had was that Charles was home at this particular point in time and could defend himself against what I was hearing. I invited them to march down to my house with me, where we found Charles with Charlita lying across the bed asleep. When he heard us come through the door, he woke up as if he had a six sense that something was wrong.

He rose up asking me, "What's wrong now, baby?" When he noticed my sisters with me, he stood up and began pacing back and forth trying to remember where he left his keys. The pacing stopped when he remembered he placed them on the dresser across the room.

It was like I was watching a bad screen play when I heard Shelia shout "tell her, tell her now how you been feeling on me!" "Yeah, me too!" said Leila. "Me too," yelled Nooky. I expected him to get upset and defend himself against their accusations, but that's not what happen. He looked them straight in the eye and smiled, glanced back at me for half a second and without one single word, before he headed out the door. His accusers feeling vindicated, decided to follow suit behind him. This heavy feeling of despair felt too familiar and I didn't like it. I shrunk into myself and started packing for the move into my new dwelling that was a good distance away from my family. I couldn't getaway fast enough.

When we were finally situated into the new habitat, I felt nothing for the house that I did the previous two weeks ago. I had reached the state when I didn't focus on anything but the welfare of my precious children. When it came to Charles, they were happy loving him and having us together. I didn't know precisely how long I could go on pretending to be content on their account. All I knew was that I had to fake it for my babies sake. As for as they knew, life was perfect.

Things were rather nice the first four weeks in the new place. Charles and I were actually behaving and enjoying each other as a happily married couple and as a good set of normal parents. I settled back into some of the routines I had when we lived next door to our old landlords, Mr. And Mrs. Gates. I have always cooked and cleaned, but I got back into the habits of baking all over again and writing poetry. Charles loved eating my delicious, homemade walnut and pecan cookies, especially when they were fresh and hot right out the oven; alongside a bowl of butter pecan ice cream. I could swear on these nights, he was the happiest man alive.

We had begun bringing the kids to the dollar movies every Friday like we used to and the kids really enjoyed it. We had done this consistently for about a month, when Charles asked if we could go to the movies the following weekend *without* the kids accompanying us. I was taken aback a little bit, but I hesitantly obliged because I knew what was coming next. I had been to Charles's job and noticed his flirtatious behavior with Pamela, one of his female co-workers. My husband never quite understood, I knew him better than he knew himself. I adamantly told myself, I was going to let this song and dance play out, hoping that I might be wrong about him. I knew that the chances were slim to none.

The next weekend arrived and we had a good time at the movies but the ride home was as I had silently predicted. Charles totally switched gears and dramatically whined about not really having the freedom he should have because he was a young father and husband. Then, he stated that he wanted to move out and live with Larry until he *found* himself. Like I said, I knew what was coming. Charles moved out the following night. When the kids asked where their daddy was, I didn't know what to say. I just promised them he'd be back soon, at least that's what I prayed anyway.

The two older kids had started school and missed their daddy an awful lot. My two younger babies weren't doing so well, either. The both of them cried all the time and refused to eat and play. I was doing my best to soothe them, but they needed him more than I could have ever imagined. One Tuesday morning, Charlita was having a crying spell that was making her sickly because she missed Charles so much. My heavenly father knew I was feeling desperate and fatigued because, out of the blue, Charles walked through our bedroom door. Right away he laid on the bed, placed her on his chest and sang her to sleep in less than 5 minutes: however, he fell asleep, too. When I came back from getting the boys from school, he was up and about working on the **transmission in my car; it needed a** new filter. He told me to change into some old clothes because he needed my help. After I aided the boys with their homework and put Charlita in her play pen, gave Cory his favorite toys, I changed clothes and under the car I went. Charles wanted me to hold up a whole car transmission, while he put in a screw. I didn't understand how this would be possible, but I did as I was told. After countless times of yelling at me because I failed at doing my assigned task, Charles got in his car and left. I was crushed and felt like I was good-for-nothing.

The next day Mama came by, picked me up, and loaned me her car so I could run errands. First, I dropped the boys off by their other grand-parents for the day. Then, I decided to pay my estranged husband an announced visit at work. That was a big mistake. When I got to Charles's job, his coworker Pamela was there, and the two of them were flirting and carrying on in front of me with the utmost disrespect. I found it to be insulting when she asked her man to buy my husband lunch. Or maybe I was over- reacting. Becoming tired of their rudeness, I stood between her and Charles and glared at him with a fury that even made the devil shudder. When he calmed the hell down and noticed me, I asked him was he coming to the house later. He said he didn't know. On that note, I quickly walked out the door to hide my tears and to diffuse my anger. I hurried to the car and drove off as fast as I could. This was the proper thing to do other than kill them both.

When I arrived at my grandmother's house where my mom was visiting, I tried to mask my frustrations as best I could. Either I did a good job at it or nobody really cared about my sadness. I was in a better mood once mama dropped me and my kids back off home for the night. After putting my babies to bed, I took a hot bubble bath. During this time, I sobbed to the Lord until I was sleepy. After hours of crying, I didn't have the energy to make it upstairs to my bedroom, so I slept on the sofa til morning. This was the first of many nights to come.

A couple days later, Charles came by the house supposedly to see the children, while driving Pamela's car. He entered the house and went straight to the bedroom where Charlita was asleep and woke her up, without even speaking to me. When I asked him why he was in Pamela's vehicle, he became upset like I was bringing up an un-necessary issue. He put Charlita down and pitched her favorite toy at our dresser mirror, breaking it before storming back out the door. He angrily told me to tell the boys he stopped by and drove the f*ck off, leaving me feeling like I overstep my bounds for asking one simple question.

After retrieving the boys from school, they were very chatty and overexcited because they were supposed to see their daddy. How was I gonna tell them, he came by already and wasn't coming back today. Needless to say, my boys became distracted and were terribly disappointed. They asked a million questions about his return and started to blame themselves for his absence. It hurt me deeply because I couldn't answer their questions or convince them that they weren't at fault for my husband's selfish neglect of being a father. As I was helping Chadrick with his homework, I became infuriated with Charles outrageousness pertaining to his selfishness. While helping Chadrick with his homework, I did the unthinkable, I struck him w**hen he answered one of his multiplication problems wrong. My poor child fell backwards,** slicing his hand open on the glass from the broken mirror his dad had shattered earlier. I wanted to kick myself for forgetting to discard the glass properly and kill myself for what I've done to my son.

It was cold and wet, as me and the children walked to the emergency room of the nearest hospital which was almost a mile away. I was holding Cory and CJ was doing his best with his baby sister. I was so upset with myself, I wanted to die. Nobody, loved my babies like I loved them, nobody. When we eventually made it to the hospital, we were seen right away. The children were cared for by an attending nurse's aide, while I was with Chadrick and the doctor. After I explained to her what happened to my son, she informed me that she might have to report me to child services because of how severe my little boy's cut was. I let her know I understood; I just wanted my son to feel better and I'd deal with the consequences later. **Once my son was discharged, the attending physician felt compassion for me and paid for us a cab ride home.** That night, I slept in bed with all my kids, promising them better days ahead.

It was another two weeks before Charles decided to come by again. This time he brought with him a dozen of beautiful long-stemmed red roses and toys for the children. I couldn't remember the last time Charles bought me flowers or the kids' toys. Nevertheless, it definitely came as a surprise. He came by and confessed that he wanted to come back home. He wanted me to give him a couple of more days to get things together and he promised he'd be the husband I deserved as well as the father our kids needed. I had been hearing this tired old speech for years, yet I continued to hope he might change: not for me but for our children. He stayed for dinner and said he had to work for the night and we would talk more about it the next day. On his way to work, I had him drop me off by my grandmother's house, where my mama was having a card game. He also took the boys over to his mom's place because it was her visiting weekend. We parted ways more pleasant than the usual, and it felt really nice. He never did ask about Chadrick's hand.

While at my grandma's home, I noticed Charlita had started running a temperature again. I called the store for Charles to let him know that I was thinking about bringing her to the ER at Children's Hospital; only to find out he wasn't there. In fact, he was off for the day. I was steaming as I fumbled with the keys, trying to start my mama's Chevette. I left Charlita with my mom as I drove to Larry's apartment to see if Charles was there. I guess the place was empty because my knocks on the door went unanswered so, I drove to where I knew Larry hung out. When I came across Larry's friends I asked if they knew where Charles could be. Their response was no, but as soon as I got back in my car, they jumped into their rides and speedily drove to Larry's place. I followed and watched them knock in vain, proving that no one really was home. I drove off and headed back to my granny's. What I saw almost killed me, literally.

I pulled up to the stoplight at the intersection, when I noticed Charles and a familiar face, two cars lengths ahead of me. I couldn't believe my eyes. With tears streaming down my face and a shroud of angriness, I pressed on the gas trying not to miss the green light, but I did. I slammed on the brakes when the light turned red, which caused me to spin out of control into oncoming traffic. I closed my eyes and waited for the impact of the automobiles to hit me but that never happened. Strangely, when I opened my eyes the vehicle was parallel parked properly behind another car on the street and someone was tapping on my window. I was amazed to see him standing there; I thought I was dreaming. I couldn't believe it was my very first admirer, Eric Joseph. He was indeed, the first guy to ever truly love me and here he was staring back at me. He slowly opened my door and helped me out of my car and into his Monte Carlo. Then we drove off into the night.

He drove and parked by a playground near the racetrack, an area of the city that was not familiar to me. After turning the car off, he slowly turned my way and addressed me, "Hey Beautiful, what's going on in your world huh? Tell me all about it." As I looked into his beautiful brown eyes, I began weeping uncontrollably. I couldn't stop my tears or extinguish the fire of pain that was burning inside of me, all the way to my soul. Once, I was able to calm down, I laid in his lap and told him all my troubles; he listened attentively, while stroking my hair. After I was all cried out, he shared with me all the reasons he fell in love with me. It was so sweet that he wanted to still take care of me, but he was married and of course I was still married, too. He begged me not to allow what I was going through to destroy all the beauty that made me a diamond in the rough. He reassured me that no matter what, he'd always love me and if he wasn't the one who was destined to take care of me, I shouldn't worry because my Romeo, my true knight in shining armor was still out there and he would find his way to me eventually. "Look up," he added. "It's written in the stars". He kissed me on my forehead before turning the key to his ignition to drive me back to my car. Eric you were my destiny I sighed quietly to myself as he drove away. Getting my head out of the clouds, I hurried back to my granny's, picked up my mother and Charlita, and dropped them both off at her home. In conclusion, I went and camped out at Charles's job and waited for him to show up.

About two hours later Charles appeared, looking like he just come off of an extended vacation. I was enraged as I walked into the mini establishment and found him in the store room, having what should have been a private phone-call. He was so busy giggling into the receiver about the good time he had last night, he didn't notice or hear me come in. When he caught a glimpse of me observing him, he almost fainted. Charles was an arrogant son of a b*tch though; he quickly gathered his composure and didn't even bother to get off the telephone with Pamela. His lack of compassion caused my heart to drop to the pit of my stomach, and instantly my head started hurting. I felt dizzy and dazed. Nothing, I mean absolutely nothing made sense to me anymore. I staggered over to the freezer and grabbed a cold grapefruit juice off the shelf and then stumbled outside teary eyed into the mist of the early morning. I painstakingly made my way over to the pay phone across the street to have a much needed woman to woman conversation with a certain female. I called Pamela and expressed to her my sorrows before making a dreadful promise that I hope she fully understood. I told her to make sure her bullsh*t work with Charles because if she didn't, I would be burning down her house with both their asses in it. I then walked back to my mom's car and went home with a sickness that no medicine could cure.

My cousin Pooch came over to look at my car the next day because he was interested in buying it and I seriously needed the money. I was struggling due to the fact that Charles hadn't given me any funds for any bills since his departure. Since Pooch was like a brother to me we settled on a price of $500, but he only gave me $100 because that was all he claimed to possess at time. I willingly trusted him to make the other two payments of $200 because he and I were close; plus he knew my situation. With the money from Pooch, I paid the light bill but I didn't know how I would manage to pay the water bill. I just couldn't seem to catch a break.

The following morning, after I had returned home from walking the kids to school, Charles showed up drunk and ran the car into the steps, putting huge dents into the cement foundation. He came up onto the porch and stood in the screened doorway yelling my name. I heard this buffoon from way upstairs while I was putting the baby back to bed. When I made it downstairs, he was standing in the kitchen barely audible and blabbing on and on about everything and nothing with an understandable apology here and there. I managed to get him back into the front room and onto the sofa to sit down, before he could pass out on the floor. "Baby, baby," he muttered repetitiously in his drunken stupor, "Come sit next to me".

I straddled him as I held his face, forcing him to look into my eyes, as I asked the one question that was going to change the dynamic of my living situation and the outcome of my children's happiness. "Are You Coming Home?" His answer was, "I can't" "Why?" I asked, looking at him purely stunned and confused.

"Becaauuse…" he slowly replied. "Bae you don't understand, the things I do to her, I could never do to you."

"Things like what?" I inquired. He began to spin me a story of how he left some Avon products at her house and she mistook it as gifts for her, so she used the items in preparations for seeing him. When he found out what she had done, he became so belligerent that he beat and sexually abused her because the products were meant for me.

The details of what he did to this woman were both sordid and savage, unlike anything I ever experienced with him. After hearing enough, I raised up off of him and he broke down like a kid caught by their parents in the act of doing something they knew was forbidden. I looked at him disgusted and embarrassed to be married to such a cruel and vicious person. I went back upstairs to make sure the baby was still asleep, before I headed out to use the payphone. As I passed Charles sleeping and snoring on the way out the door, I rushed to the payphone six blocks away. Upon reaching my destination, I took a minute to catch my breath before I made my call. Then I dialed the number.

"Hello, may I speak to Pamela?"

When she stated it was her speaking, I immediately dove into my big sister sympathy speech.

"Why? Why? Why, are you letting Charles, a married man mistreat you so badly? Beating you and degrading your body over what? Some freaking Avon? Despite the circumstances, Pamela, no woman deserves to be treated like that. Charles has never treated me like that.

You can do better, so much better! "You hear me?" I screamed into the phone.

"But I love him, Anita" she answered.

I dropped the receiver, shook my head and trotted home. I genuinely felt sorry for her.

WHAT DO YOU SEE?

CHARLES CAME BY to pick the kids up this morning. He said that he is sober, but I smelled alcohol on his breath, although the odor was faint. After they were gone, I paced almost the entire duration of the four and a half hours my baby girl was absent from me. I didn't worry about the boys too much because I knew they were going to end up by Ms. Lynn before he returned. But my baby, that's a different story altogether. When he brought my baby home, he proceeded to amusingly tell me how he took Charlita over to Pamela's house and she broke the woman's nose. Before I could ask the question, he blurted out the answer; she hit her in the face with her rattle. He jokingly swore that the baby had an intuition, that Pamela was her mama's competition. I told him he was stupid as I took my daughter out of his arms, stating, "I thought you would have been proud," he taunted.

I bid him a good day before abruptly closing my door in his face. Exasperated, I flopped onto the sofa with my daughter and began talking to her.

"Hey there, Mama's pretty girl", I crooned to my darling six-month-old. In between her laughs, she tried to bite my cheeks, which made my heart flutter. This had become a habit of hers since she was two months old, but she was still unsuccessful. Her two bottom teeth didn't even change the outcome of her slobbery attempts. My perfect little miracle always made things a whole lot more tolerable, no matter how difficult situations became. This made me love her more with each passing second. I was glad I had my baby girl to comfort me because we had received a second eviction notice. We had to be out of the house in 3 days.

I moved back in with my mama and my daddy yet again and I hated it. I was a married woman, with 4 kids; it wasn't supposed to be like this. Charles was making a fool of me and a mockery of the marriage that I promised God I'd deal with for a lifetime. He never intended to make things right since the f*cked up day that he showed up to marry me. I couldn't process what was happening to me, so, I decided to take a vacation to the country and visit my sweet great-grandmother Inez. I told my mama my plans and asked her to make sure my boys attended school regularly and to keep me in her prayers. I packed luggage for Charlita, Cory and myself and, just like that I was on my way to where I perceived I'd find the answers to the queries that were devastating my life.

After the first couple of nights of being in the middle of no-where, I came up with an idea to make a diary about important details and pertinent memories about my irrational life. These occurrences have affected and, to some degree, molded me as this strange, obstinate individual. I hoped my babies would get to read these few pages of my existence, when they are all grown-up.

Ever since I can remember, I've always known I was kind of different. No matter what went on around me, I always managed to stand out somehow, whether it was by my choice or not. We didn't have much growing up before my mama got married, but she made do. I remember being 5 years old, always eager and ready to go to school. Unfortunately, in kindergarten I was teased by my older peers because I didn't have much hair. I hated myself even more when I lost my teeth. So, one day I went to school with my grandmother's false teeth in my mouth, along with her wig on my head. My teacher was sweet and kind as she combed my very short hair into a tiny, tiny Afro and placed my granny's teeth into a plastic bag. She did these things before calling my mother with the news that I'd borrowed granny's things without permission. Who thought growing up was easy? Me, that's who.

W*hile I was at school,* I really enjoyed playing with the toys. It was the only time where I got to live out my fantasies of being rich and beautiful. I often pretended the stuff animals and dolls were my friends. I liked to play all by my lonesome with no interruptions from anyone and without judgement. I had a special liking for a tall white naked doll, I named Mary; she was my best friend. One morning I went to school and no students were there other than myself and I had no idea why. I went to my classroom as always and waited but none of the kids ever arrived. After playing with Ms. Mary for a while longer, I decided to go back home but I was not going alone. When I made it home, I found my mama and my relatives all searching for me. There I was holding a big white doll as tall as me looking lost as to what all the fuss was about. Well turns out the reason why I didn't see any other students was because we didn't have school, due to winter break. Shortly, after I walked through the front door, my mama received a phone call from my teacher. She informed her that I had to return Ms. Mary back to her rightful place. This left me feeling really blue, but I found comfort in knowing that I'd be reunited with Ms. Mary after the holidays were over.

I always had the gift of sight or prophetic vision since I was 5 years old. I didn't fully grasp what to call it at the time. I recalled having this recurring dream of me being covered in crimson and surrounded by people in all white. I woke up every night scared out of my mind. Well, what I saw eventually came true. I graduated from kindergarten the following month in red and the other graduates were dressed in white, of course. The dream didn't ring any bells to me at this age as something to be considered unique or special at time.

Like many others, I was molested at this tender age also. I won't feed into the stereo type of being considered a victim because I survived it. As a matter of fact, I won't give any sordid details because I don't want to be pitied or have to relive that trauma. How-ever, I will say that enduring this pain prepared me for the strength to withstand anything. It made me recognize all the beauty that existed in everything surrounds us. Don't get me wrong, it wasn't something that I asked for but it made me realize early on in life that there is evil in the world and it seemed to have it sights set on destroying me. Knowing this forced me to examine all that ever stood between me and my happiness. But it's evident and obvious that even though I am armed with this knowledge, I was doomed to fail at a lot of things: like for instance, being a wife.

I grew up around bar-rooms because my grandmother and one of her sisters were the proprietors of a few. I can still remember the day I was at my great- aunt Sylvia's bar and a man was shot across the street in front of his mechanic shop. I could swear I saw his spirit staring back at me and pointing toward my direction from beyond the grave. Then all of a sudden, he was beside me and I heard him whisper in my ear very clearly, "Tell the world, death is not the end!" And just like that, he was gone.

The next troubling dream or vision I had involved my favorite cousin getting hit by a car. Two days later, just like I dreamed, he and I were racing across the street when suddenly a vehicle struck him, knocking him several feet into the air before he made a crashing thud with the pavement. I was scared that I had lost him forever, but if I had remembered the whole dream, I would have known that he would make a full recovery. Well, almost a full recovery.

My family was into the card game scene; it was their way of spending time together, accumulate funds to pay bills, and a way to temporarily forget their troubles. I never knocked my mama's hustle, but it was never something I took interest in. Due to mama excessive card playing, I had a lot of free time to study all sorts of people and I learn to see God in everything. I learned early on in life that everyone has a certain degree of good and a certain degree of bad inside of them. One just overpowers the other.

I tried to stay out of sight, even though I saw and heard more than the average kid my age should have. By the time my mama got with my daddy, my siblings and I had our own way of co-existing. We practically did everything together. When my daddy came into our lives, my world was turned and flipped upside down. Back then,

I didn't understand nothing about the man, except he was so darn surly. When he entered our lives on a daily basis, things changed for both, better and worse. We had more of life's comforts, but at a price that has stigmatized the Riley clan forever.

By the time I was seven years old, things began to stir inside of me that were quite unsettling and calming at the same time. Different events brought about different emotions. I was in second grade and I'll never forget the day I ran home from school with a lovely pink crochet hen that I won from a dance contest during our back to school party. When I gave it to mama, she was so proud of it, but I know I hurt her feelings by taking it out the china cabinet where she had placed it, and then gave it to my aunt/god-mother. At the time, I didn't understand why I did this. I was genuinely sorry for hurting her though. At 7, kids were beginning to become very cruel. My schoolmates nicknamed me Pissy Girl. I was beginning to hate school because of the bullying and teasing I experienced.

There was one person who did not tease me and his name was Johnny Mathews. He made sure to sit by me every day at our designated table at lunch time. One day before school was dismissed, I asked Johnny for his home number to talk with him later. That night I called him about 8:00pm, thinking my parents wouldn't be the wiser. I don't know the full content of the phone call with the exception of me asking him do he know what I want. His reply was, "Tell me." I answered by spelling, D * C K! Then he asked me if I knew what he wanted? I replied, "No, what? He responded by loudly spelling out P * S S Y! I had no idea how long my parents had been listening in on my phone conversation. After they finally heard enough they gave me what they thought I needed, a good butt whipping. I don't think they honestly and truly assessed the ramifications of what living next door to an Adult X-Rated theater would have upon us as small children. Watching the contents of those movies when they would air out the theater during certain times of the month contributed to me making a lot of bad decisions in my life.

At that delicate age of my life, I was torn over the lack of empathy that the kids around me possessed. There were a couple of girls that shared the same last name I did which was Smith. They made me feel like I was a piece of diseased sh*t that they just so happen to share the same last name as. I came up with this great plan to win over the favor of my classmates that was sure to make me popular and thwart off the thoughts I had of wishing myself dead. I decided that since Rev. Riley spoiled my mama with so much, why not share the wealth? My teacher's birthday was coming up in a week or so and we were planning to throw her a big surprise party around the same time we would be celebrating Halloween. *I went into my mother's closet and took two sets of her expensive Egyptian sheets to give to Ms. Turner as agift from me and my classmates.*

Oh! I didn't do it just once, I did it on several different occasions. I added new towels, along with the sheetsets. I even gave her a baby coat that belonged to my little god brother. Unfortunately, when my step-dad found out, he went ballistic and marched me right up to the school and embarrassed the hell out of me in front of the teacher, the principal and the entire class. He shamed me in front of everybody telling them I needed to have my brain checked out because only a crazy person would do something so, well, crazy. He never bothered asking me why I did it? If he would have, he might have maybe, just maybe understood what I was going through.

Right after that incident, things became much worse for me. The kids were meaner than ever and now they were beating on me. The first vicious act of violence came from my best friend, Linda Cartwright; at least I thought we were best friends. She was still griping because I got Ms. Turner into a whole lot of trouble. I thought that if nobody else could forgive me she would, but she had become my biggest adversary. It was the following week after Ms. Turner had returned the last and final gift when the class expressed their anger by calling me names, pitching objects at the back of my head and shooting spitballs in my face. I tapped Linda on the shoulder and asked her if she was still mad at me, too? She didn't turn to face me but mumbled something that I didn't quite understand. Then I remembered that it was her birthday and I tapped her on her shoulder once more. when I did this, she stood up over me while I was still seated and bombarded me with a slew of unsolicited shots across my face that had the class applauding and cheering with great excitement and appreciation. I was in complete shock. So much so, that I couldn't move my limbs because they felt really heavy. All I could do was put my head down on the desk and quietly weep. It goes without saying that I felt like I wanted to be anywhere other than where I was for the moment. I was stumped for answers, but I knew they would eventually find me. I'm talking about patience and faith; they were always my true friends, even then.

When I was nine, my mama had another baby, my little brother. He felt more like my own child because he was always with me. My parents made this baby my life. I wasn't the cleanest girl going to school and I did reek of urine because some of my siblings wet the bed. How-ever,I vowed to be the best big sister that my siblings, especially my new baby brother could ever have. After all, God himself placed me in this role, not them.

I remember going to school and we had a surprise visit from the school nurse. Her name was Ms.Wade and she was there to give us a physical. I vividly can recall not wanting to get undressed in front of the other girls. I pretended to be sick, which only made matters worse for me. Noticing that the other girls were clearly picking on me, Nurse Wade decided to save my examination for last. When she realized my reluctance to take off my already stained clothing, she immediately gravitated to me and gave me the biggest hug. When I finally stripped down to my underwear, they were not the cleanest, but they smelled somewhat fresh. She knew right away that my circumstances were somewhat tough. She recognized that I had honor and self-preservation, which meant everything to me. She gave me my examination and we departed with a mutual respect for one another. It was around this time that I thought I understood my value and self-worth.

My mama finally was due to marry my step-dad, but I wasn't

chosen to be in the wedding. I knew she was going to make a beautiful bride and I couldn't wait to see her in her dress. When the wedding day arrived, everybody was so excited. I wasn't too excited because my mother dressed me in the ugliest shade of orange. My mama loved dressing me in orange and I still don't know why. I remember someone had asked the bridal party why I was not getting primped up for the wedding. One of my relatives blurted out that I wasn't getting primped because I was not marching. The person who asked the question persistently asked why not? My relative responded by alluding to my less than beautiful features being the reason for my non-participation. Her remarks made me cry, so I ran outside and sat on the porch.

Shortly afterwards, the wedding party was ready to depart. I ran inside to get my baby brother's diaper bag and stroller. When I came back out the limo and everyone were gone, except my sister, Joyce. Joyce was my first little sister and she was my best friend. I knew she wouldn't have left without me. We were sitting on the steps of my great-aunt's beauty salon, when my uncle's wife, Lilian. spotted us and immediately stopped and picked us up. She said jokingly, that's it's a good thing she 's never on time for anything or else she wouldn't have been able to rescue us.. When we finally made it the wedding, we had missed the vow exchange and everyone was headed to the reception. One of my aunts handed me my baby brother and I spent the rest of the day trying to nurse him back to health; he was sick with diarrhea, a fever and very colicky. I didn't get to really see mama in her dress or any of the activities that went along with the wedding. I didn't even get to enjoy a plate of food, or something cold to drink. I was so happy when the festivity had ended. I was ready to get in my bed and go to sleep.

After my mama and step-dad got married, we started going to church non-stop. Our parents made us join the choir and junior usher board. **On most Sundays,** I was made an assistant Sunday school teacher alongside my step-daddy. It was evident that I was going to be an instrument for the LORD, whether I wanted to be or not. I wished I had as much attention paid to me in other areas of my life as I did when it came to church.

WHERE IS YOUR FAITH?

I WAS LOST in thought, reflecting on my childhood, when my uncle Willie came in the room and asked me "Do you want to go for a ride, Niece?"

Since my mind had grown weary and my baby wasn't sleepy yet, I answered him with a very enthusiastic, "Heck yeah!"

That was the first night I realized how dark it really got in the heart of the country because there were no street lamps. We all hopped in Uncle Willie's jalopy and drove up the road, around a curve and came to a sudden halt. I assumed we ran out of gas in the middle of nowhere, but we were actually at someone's house. With the honking of Uncle Willie's car horn, on came lights and in an instant, I was looking at the silhouette of a house that looked like it existed since the slave era.

"Well I'll be! Hey there, Willie! Whatcha doin' here?" Those words slurred from the mouth of a woman who was as sweet as apple pie.

"Well now Hattie Mae, I thought this person might interest ya," said Uncle Willie. He went on, "This here's yo niece Nitra. This yo brother Junny daughter and her two young-ins".

She gave me the biggest hug ever and fell in love with Charlita at first sight. She grabbed Cory from my arms, declaring he looked like her baby brotha Warren. She invited us inside her little shack and told me stories about the man that was my daddy and my mama. She told me how she wish she knew I existed because it genuinely broke her heart to have someone look just like her that she was related to and didn't have the pleasure of knowing. After leaving Aunt Hattie Mae's home, we headed back into town to Sonic's Drive Thru. Uncle Willie bought us hamburger combos and shakes. After we ate, we chugged our way back to the center of no man's land.

The next day my mama's best friend, Lizzy Ann, came by my granny's to see and fetch me and my babies. I always loved Aunt Lizzy. She had a country accent that gave me an instant high. She brought me and my kids to her house which was in town. Once we got there, she cooked us a nice dinner and rented us a few movies to watch. We were having a great time enjoying the movie Ghost Busters, when Aunt Lizzy got an emergency phone call from her job and had to leave right away. She insisted that we continue watching the movie without her and she'd be back as soon as she could. During the middle of the second movie, my younger cousins who had come over to meet me had fallen asleep: my babes were knocked out, too. My older cousin, Pop, and I stayed up discussing our relationship issues for a while, and then cleaned the kitchen before heading for bed too. Early that morning, my 8 month old woke me up by hitting me repeatedly across the forehead with her bottle. She wanted me to become aware of the new stranger in the room.. When I popped open my eyes, before me stood an older gentleman I'd never seen before. He looked just like a cowboy straight out the magazines. He smiled and then asked me, "Do you know who I am?"

"Yes Sir, You are Junny, my daddy." I casually replied.

"That's right" he coolly stated. "Come give yo daddy a hug, gal". I slowly rose up to stand and without a moment's notice, ran into his arms. I had wanted to do this for such a long time and it was worth the wait. My daddy took me to his apartment where I met his fian'ce Susan, along with the gang of siblings, I didn't know I had. Sadly, just as quickly as Junny came, he was gone because he was living and working in Texas. Aunt Lizzy called and told him about me being there and he drove all night from Houston to Lake Portia to come and meet me. Before he left though, he told me to stay with Susan and if I was in need of anything, not to hesitate to call him.. Susan did all she could to make me feel comfortable and welcomed.. She tried to help me forget my troubles, but it became virtually impossible. My mama called me just about every hour to update me on every move Charles was making with and without Pamela. She had no clue her information was causing me to become sicker and sicker. It was evident that my trip to the country wasn't going to make me feel any better, but the distance away from my husband and his mistress was saving their lives and they didn't even know it.

After being in the country for almost two months, I had to get back home to my other two children, whom I missed terribly. That weekend, I bid my new-found family a farewell and headed back to the city. The closer the train got to New Orleans, the more I began dreading returning home. Mama came and picked me up with the boys and I was so excited to see them as they bum rushed me with enough kisses and hugs to last me a life time. I immediately became upset upon learning that my children had not been attending school on a regular basis: since my departure. I really regretted leaving them behind because I knew no one could or would care for them like me. I won't ever make that mistake again.

Mama invited me to go with her over to my grandma's place for a short visit, but it turned out to be a card game. I was in no mood for a damn card game. My family appeared genuinely happy to see me, and I must admit, the feeling was mutual. The feeling was mutual, until they decided to address my marital affairs. A few of them eagerly gossiped about seeing Charles in different places with Pamela. My husband plaything lived only a few hundred feet from my granny's doorstep. My grandma admitted that they all knew he practically was living with her now.. I commented on how he was mistreating me for some ugly wench that didn't equal to me in no area when it came to being a woman. My granny stopped dealing cards for a moment, looked up at me and said "Baby, ugly people need love too", then went back to dealing cards. With family and guest all agreeing with my grandmother's wisdom, I immediately began to feel smaller and smaller and more insignificant. I abruptly gathered my children and left. I just wanted to find my place, the place where I truly belong. The place where I mattered, where my feelings were important, where I didn't have to hide behind a fake smile. I wanted to feel the genuine acceptance and love I got from my family in the country. I just wanted to feel happy and safe. I wanted my children to know unconditional love not just from me but others too..

A couple of weeks later, mama had her whole troop together with the exception of Franklin Jr. all at Sonnies Cool Spot, the bar around the corner from the house. Everybody with the exception of myself were enjoying themselves drinking and shooting pool, when in walk this guy that was a stranger to us all, yet familiar to me. He was listening to my family mockingly rambling about the troubles, injustices and misfortunes that befell their lives, when he unwittingly interjected himself into their mischief. "So tell us my brother what have you been through?" mocked John, with a sly grin running across his face as wide as the Mississippi River. The young man, realizing his mistake, didn't give any hint or clues to what his distresses were. Instead he beat the crap out of John in a game of billiards, with a smile of his own. After his win, he came and had a seat near the bar and asked me what I was drinking?

"Heineken beer with a Pepsi," I answered in a really dry and unenthusiastic tone. "In the same cup? Together?" he grinned.

"Yep," I replied while taking a quick sip.

"What's your name, young lady?" he pleasantly inquired.

I responded by saying "Before I give you my name, let me tell you something. I need a friend. Will you be my friend?"

He held out his hand and said, "Hi, I'm Casey."

"Hi, Casey, Nice to meet you," I sweetly replied.

After the bar closed, he and I walked down the opposite block of my house and set on a neighbor's stoop, there we talked until the break of dawn. He did not want us to part ways but it was unavoidable. Casey made me feel wanted, something I really missed feeling. The last time I felt desirable, I was with Eric.. Before Casey hesitantly left my side, he made a promise to meet me at the bar later on during the evening, then, he sprinted off toward his home. I slowly walked to my abode, feeling blissful and restored. I soon realized I told Casey a whole lot about my current state of affairs, but I never shared my name. I took a warm bath and thought about this stranger way more than I should have. I didn't know what I was getting myself into, but I would soon find out.

Later on that evening Casey met me at the bar, just like he promised. His promptness and the fact that he was true to his word made me feel valid and joyful. *Our surroundings became void* as we engaged in more conversation about ourselves and what we desired for those who were attached to our lives. We left the bar again, in the wee hours of the morning, and went to Joyce house. Although we were grown adults, we found ourselves making out and carrying on like silly teenagers. I discovered it to be strange that he;didn't want to have sex with me. This had me puzzled and I I didn't know if that was a good thing or bad thing:, I was really confused. He must have read the look on my face because he reassured me that he was interested in me in every way, but that it was not the right time for us to become intimate. He told me not to worry because he wasn't going anywhere. We kissed another five or ten minutes and then he was gone.

The day Casey came to meet my babies was one of the most mortifying and blessed days of my life. I didn't have any electricity, because I couldn't afford to pay the high energy bill, so my lights were turned off that morning. As if I could handle another issue, I got a visit from Child Protection Services investigating the report of abuse from the request of the physician that saw Chadrick when his hand was cut a few months back. Casey and the worker from CPS arrived at my front door at almost the exact same time: Thank God Casey came only seconds before she did. Before she could ask me one single question Casey asked if he could talk with her alone for a moment. Right away they went outside to converse privately. To this very day, I have no idea what he told her, but she left and I never heard from her again. I owed Casey so much for handling this crisis for me, and boy did I pay for it!

Sonnies became my second home, that's where I discovered my love for shooting pool. As for Mr.Casey, he became my alternate conquest,The first night Casey had decided to stay over, I thought he finally wanted to have intercourse but that was not his intentions at all. He stayed over to help me with Charlita and to assist me with my daddy, who, at this time, had lost his legs due to diabetic complications. .I made up my mind that I was going to make Casey love me tonight but he still insisted it wasn't the right time:. I gave up and went to sleep. Early the next morning we were awaken by hard knocks on the back door and the side of the house. Casey groggily asked me if I wanted him to answer the door?. I I sleepily responded. I headed to the front of the house and unwittingly opened the door,, thinking it was a relative, but it was Charles: he was drunk as usual. I tried to close the door,back but he pushed pass me like he could smell a someone else in the house with me. He raced to the rear bedroom of the residence and attacked Casey: who was still asleep..I ran in pursuit of Charles and had barely made it to the room in time to save my baby from being trampled by the two of them. During their violent struggle, I made a beeline to the front of the house to get help from my family on the other side of the duplex. I was grateful that they were awakened by the commotion and were already two steps ahead of me.

Before I could place Charlita on the bed next door,Charles happened to appear and had the nerve to slap me across the face. I had put up with a lot of sh*t from Charles, but hitting me in my face was definitely a line that he shouldn't have crossed. My mama came in like Hank Aaron, waving a two by four while daring him to strike me again, then the police walked in. It was comical yet frightening all at once. After hearing the details of what took place, the cops tried to pacify the situation by making Charles the victim. I was pissed at them and worried about Casey all at the same time. I had no idea where or how my friend was doing. I found out my family thought it was a good decison to lock him in the house next door for his safety.

When he was released, from his temporary confinement, the cops took his statements then they asked if he desired to press charges against Charles, for assault and battery. He declined, saying he could really understand a husband's reaction in learning that his wife has moved on. He then stated he was more concerned about me and wanted to know my where-abouts..When he walked through the door all bloody, I felt so bad, but the first thing he did was come to comfort me. He gently rubbed the area where Charles slapped me and then asked me if I was OK? All I could do was shake my head yes while whispering my apologies to him. It was becoming increasingly difficult to fight back my tears. When the police asked me about pressing charges, my answer was very different from Casey's. They took Charles's ass to jail, but not before Casey got his revenge. As Charles watched Casey plant kisses all over his daughters tiny hands and face, tears swelled in his eyes. Upon seeing Charles cry my family asked me to have a change of heart regarding his future destination. I remained obstinate with my course of action. The last thing Charles saw before the police drove off was Casey making his daughter wave bye-bye to him. This tugged at my heart just a little, until, I remembered him striking my cheek. I hoped a little time in jail would be a wake up call for him to stop drinking.

Larry bailed Charles out within hours with a stern warning, "Stay The Hell Away From Anita!" Charles came by the next day and saw Casey playing football in the street with the boys. It ate him alive to see someone doing what he should have been doing.."Nita I know you fed up, I know, but I'm ready to come home," he uttered, as if I hadn't heard it all before. After standing in his company for about an hour I went to retrieve the baby for him. She didn't want to see him and it was his own fault for not coming around often enough to visit her. Even the boys were to distracted to entertain him. As he sadly drove away I began to feel pity for him...

New Years Eve of 1990 was a day full of unexpectancy for me. Casey and I were dressed in black jeans and white sweatshirts, enjoying ourselves at Sonnies bar with the family when someone came to inform me that my husband wanted me outside, Agh, no! Not this sh*t again! When I shared this information with Casey, he advised me to take ten minutes to hear him out, only because it was New Year's eve. He said if I was gone for too long, he'd come outside to get me personally. Still, I hesitantly agreed and I headed out the door to meet up with Charles against my better judgement.

Charles was parked in front of my door, waiting on me to come from around the corner. He started the car and met up with me before I was half way up the block. When he stopped the car I got in with a horrendous feeling. We drove around the neighborhood for about twenty minutes before a single word was said. I became irritated and impatient and wanted to return back to my company and then I found out why it was so important for us to meet. Charles had a nine milometer glock in his right hand that he waved before my face for a few minutes then, laid his hand with the gun back down on the seat. Then he spoke in a drunken tirade about killing me plus himself. I stared at Charles for a moment, then my surroundings, then back at Charles again. I became very angry and screamed "You can kill your f*ucking self!" Then, I jumped out the moving car and ran all the way back to Sonnies. When I went into the bar I immediately shared with everybody what happened!. The response I received was a heap of nonchalance. Casey took me outside and calmed me down and decided that we should return to the house and let the New Year catch us there. That was very considerate and good thinking on his part, so home I went. We brought the New Year in making love.

Things between Casey and me were good for a while, but out of nowhere, our relationship took a tumultuous turn. When it came to treating me like a lady he was perfect, but financially, he was crap. Charles and I were really estranged now, the kids were the only thing we had in common. I was making love to just one man and it wasn't my husband. In hindsight I was relieved, but for the most part I felt so worthless in the eyesight of God. Because of Casey I struggled greatly with regaining my connection back to God.

I struggled to establish boundaries with Charles and with Casey.

I went back and forth with these two for months before I finally decided to allow Charles to move back in. I only did so on the strength of our boys and their love for him. Charles was still unemployed, but seemed to be searching adamantly for another job. Then, one day he came home with this sh*t storm of an idea. He said he ran into some guy at a seminar that promised him that he could make a good salary selling picture packages at local department stores. He said that he would be traveling out of state and the only thing he needed to do was come out of pocket for his own personal lodging and food. He proceeded to tell me that everything else would be paid for by the company, which didn't have a name. I wanted to slap Charles across the face to wake him up out of this get rich quick scheme that was nothing but a mere rip off. Because he was convinced it was the real thing, I gave into his foolishness. All it required was my last bit of money $450.00 to make all our woes to go away. Later on that night, Charles left for Florida.

Meanwhile, Theresa popped up at the house to see how I was doing. She patiently listened while I bi*tched about my bank account being empty and my kids being hungry all day. To make matters worse, I hadn't heard anything from Charles, either. Theresa, being the bad influence she always have been, talked me into writing checks to Pizza Hut and Dominoes to feed the kids for almost a week. She also suggested I go to the Office of Family support to get food stamps and my checks reinstated, until Charles could provide on a more stable basis. I knew she was right, so I took her advice and did what was best for my children, instead of depending on the promises of a broken man. When I did hear from Charles again, he shared that he'd be home sooner than expected because things didn't work out according to plan. In the back of my mind, I always believed he went to visit his old beau from his military days and things didn't go as he hoped. Charles was a dog like that. He didn't send or come back with a red cent. I had to take my government assistance and pay the DA for bounced checks, a total of $527.81. Being with Charles sometimes made me question my sanity.

My daddy was now admitted in the hospital and calling me sub-consciously. I heard him day in and day out. He needed to see me but I didn't want to go visit him because I knew I had to say goodbye and I'm no good at saying goodbye. I was tired, but I promised myself I'd go see him later after I took a nap. I dreamed a dream of dreams: my past, my present and my future. Nobody would ever believe my daddy and I were dreaming the same dream at the exact same time. Once I awoke, Charles and I made the journey to the hospital for me to see my daddy. As I was walking through the doors of the ICU, he was calling my name. "It's me, Daddy," I answered. I walked over to the bed and kissed him on the forehead as I took hold of his hand. He began to tell me about his dream and suddenly stopped and said,

"I forgot. You were there right, Nita?"

"Right, daddy", I laughed as I let my tears freely fall. I pulled up a chair and began a heart felt conversation with him. I started our talk by asking for his forgiveness. I needed him to beg my pardon for dis-respecting him, for running away from home, for not living up to my fullest potential, for not fully representing the duty of a true preacher's daughter and for trying to kill him when I was younger.

"He, in turn, told me to stand up and put my ear to his mouth and he tearfully declared," You are forgiven. You are truly special and I should have treated you like so. I beg your pardon, too. I should never done a lot of things I did. I could have pruned you better for the Lord and I'm so sorry I messed that up, but daddy do love you." He further went on to say that I was different, and a good person and to remem-ber what he taught me. "Shape your nose," as he shaped my nose for the last time. He asked Charles to pray for him.

"I can't, I don't know how, Mr. Riley," he painstakingly admitted.

"I'll pray for you, Daddy," I insisted. It was the first and last time my daddy ever heard me pray out loud to the father, the *Anita way*. For the first time I knew my daddy was really pleased with me. Five minutes after Charles and I arrived back home from the hospital, we received the call. My daddy had passed away. It is funny how nobody even knew we had been there to see him and that was somehow OK with me.

For daddy's funeral, our family and friends were breaking down, barely maintaining any form of self-control. I really had to hold it together, especially for my mama and my siblings. My daddy had a lot of people that loved and cared about him. My sister Sheila was really in denial about daddy's death. When the casket was put into the grave site, she just lost it. It took me and Quan, her boyfriend to help her regain some sense of composure and realize she couldn't bring daddy back or bring him home. It took some time, but we were able to accomplish this thwarting task. I was at peace with Daddy's death because he really suffered tremendously and I pictured him in heaven, happy and having a beer with his old buddy, Mr. Greg.

It wasn't until we were on our way back from the re-pass dinner that I truly learned how much I genuinely detested my spouse. I thought I could finally be vulnerable and breakdown to Charles concerning my father's death. I was wrong as usual. Just when I was about to speak, this son of a b*tch starts to cry over my pops. He was blabbing about a whole bunch of things that I wasn't interested in hearing. I was totally out done. When the limo ultimately stopped in front of the house, I thanked the driver, grabbed my kids and marched inside and slammed the door in his face. This was the day I accepted and comprehended that my faults were fixable, but I couldn't repair other people's stupidity. Perhaps, I could only learn from it. I was never truly granted the chance to grieve over my daddy. Not once! After daddy's burial, I truly didn't want Charles around me on a permanent basis any more. The only people content and delighted with his presence were my family and the kids.

To appease my frustration and unhappiness, I decided to go out with my Aunt Ruthie. We went to watch her male friend and his live band perform at a very popular upscale nightclub, not too far from the house. I figured it would be a stimulating experience and it absolutely was. When the band played and the singers sang, they drew you into something completely new and familiar, all at once! Their act, caused a delightful disturbance inside of you that was nostalgic. I had such a wonderful time with my aunt, I promised her we'd do it again real soon and we did. I went out with my aunt on two more occasions to hear the band play. It was the ending of the third evening that was the beginning of great suffering for me. There was a band member named Travis that was really close to my aunt who volunteered to drop the both of us off at our separate homes. Because my aunt lived closer to the club, he took her home first.

As he pulled up in front of my door, I thanked him and exited the car laughing at the joke he made about Charles standing in the doorway, waiting for me. When I reached the door way I knew the night was not going to end peacefully for me. **The look in his eyes was the same look Jimmy had the night he walked up on me with his gun.** Charles was drunk and was making all kinds of accusations about me revenge cheating on him. Before I could defend myself, we inadversely began to tussle and fight throughout the duplex. Upon realizing this, I fought back even harder, knowing I shouldn't have. Charles being heightened in rage picked me up by my neck and choke slammed me down across the corner of our black lacquer dresser. His actions caused a deep gash to my inner thigh as my parted legs and mangled body hit the floor. When he finished his brutal examination of my vagina with his oversized manhood, he passed out and I just laid there too battered to move. Little did I know, the combination of alcohol and violence would become a practice that he would eventually perfect.

When morning arrived, I awoke in the same spot Charles left me. I screamed out in pain,as I climbed into the tub to soak my aching body. Although I knew what my husband had just put me through was barbaric, I couldn't help but wonder if it was justice served for all the times I cheated with Casey. To think I could equal myself with a man on that level was very foolish thinking. To my sorrows, at the end of the day, I was still Mrs. Charles Duke.

The following weekend, I was on my way to Texas with my biological dad, Junny. He was truly a funny character. He was someone that I really had a good time with, no matter where we were. I could listen to him talk all day and his laugh was so contagious. On our journey to Texas, we had three different tires to blowout. Junny said he never experienced nothing so bizarre. "Nitra, you might be bad luck," he joked. When we finally reached our destination, I was in disbelief with how big Houston was. In my opinion, you could fit the entire state of Louisiana inside of Houston.

I was in Houston enjoying myself, all of 24 hours, when Charles and my mama showed up. The peace and refuge I felt quickly vaporized into thin air the moment I heard husband's voice. I couldn't believe he was there. I really just couldn't believe it. I was so troubled, I couldn't even cry anymore. I couldn't get away from him. He was destined to haunt and hunt me no matter where I was or would be. My uncle Ryan asked me if I was okay, before we left and returned back to Louisiana the following morning. I put on a pretend smile and did my best to assure him everything was good and that I'd see again in the near future. Because I hated to leave, I took my time to enter the vehicle. As we were driving off, I decided not to glance back at my family waving us good-bye. I knew if I did, I would have to acknowledge that once again, I would be on the highway heading back to where I didn't want to be.

When we made it home again, I sunk into a deep depression. I could no longer masquerade my unhappiness for the sake of the kids anymore. Deep down inside, I was screaming for a way out of this built in hell in which I dwelled, but I didn't know where to find the master key. I was grateful Charles decided to spend a few days with his mama because I was making him miserable. If that ain't the pot calling the kettle black. I finally would have some time away from his abusive, drunken stupors which he didn't remember because he would drink until he blacked out. I couldn't forget though and it was so unfair. I took comfort in knowing that retribution would visit him someday. I knew firsthand that God had a way of righting our wrongs. Charles showed back up a few days later, desiring to make a fresh start again, as usual. Shockingly for the first time ever, he wanted to make a mid-week visit to our dear friends, Charles and Lana. With the state of mind I was in, nothing mattered anymore. The last time

I saw Lana I was pregnant with my little girl. I was anxious for our friends to meet my little girl; she was amazing. Nothing could stop the tiny twinge of hope that seemed to somehow jump start my heart whenever she smiled at me. My daughter and the highway were the antidotes that cured my melancholy, but only on a temporary basis. I looked to the future for a more permanent solution.

While visiting our friends, I actually was enjoying myself. Spending time with both Lana and the baby, was just what I needed. I always felt at ease in the country setting; something about the air was gratifying to me. It gave me a sense of tranquility as I contemplated about finding my true purpose. If I could only gather the strength to walk in that purpose, my existence wouldn't feel or be so meager. If I had a true dependable ally, I knew my future wouldn't look so grim or appear so bleak. I was born tenacious and resilient. I have always been a survivor, but I wanted to do more than survive. I wanted to en-joy living on my own terms, without the leash or the harness that my husband controlled. I wanted to feel the same freedom in the city that I adored in the country. That freedom made me believe I could be and achieve anything. It made me believe I was destined to be more than a mother and an unhappy wife. I was not destined to die miserable. I just could not accept that as my fate.

For the first time, Lana and I, along with our husbands, went to the mall and shopped. It was a welcomed distraction from our routine chaotic lives. Charles wandered off from me for a short span only to return frantic. He apologized after informing our friends that he and I had to depart in a hurry. He also promised that we would check in with them later. Within a flash, we were headed back home way sooner than I had anticipated. My spouse didn't drop a hint or give me a clue why we were leaving so soon.. He was definitely nervous and agitated about something, so I didn't press him for any informa-tion. I decided to keep my mouth close and my eyes on the road as we drove home in silence.

Charles pulled up in front of the house, told me to pack up every-thing to go into storage and to make sure I get the boys whatever they would need for the course of a couple of weeks. Then he casually included that he'd be back in a couple of days. Once I was out the car with the baby, he drove madly down the block and turned the corner out of sight with-in a matter of seconds. I walked up the steps to my side of the duplex, completely worn out. I collapsed on my sofa and called Casey and confided in him all my troubles.

After chatting about thirty minutes with him, I dozed off and was awakened by a hard knock at the door; to my surprise, it was Patrick and his cousin, Wayne. Charles apparently sent them with a U-haul moving truck to load all our things into, before heading over to the storage facility. I asked Patrick did he have an idea why Charles was acting so erractic? He looked me in the eye and lied, "No, Nita I don't." While they were moving the furniture, I packed my kids things and started on their dinner. When Joyce came by to check on me I was more than elated to have her company. Now I had someone to help me with the kids while I tried to organize a hundred other things. When my sister asked where I was moving to, I couldn't give her a definitive answer. So, I just changed the subject.

While Joyce was standing outside on the porch talking with Patrick, she called me to the door. "You know him?" she asked.

"Who?" I asked her in return.

"That dude driving the convertible car," she replied.

"Oh sh*t! Nita, I think that's Snake Eyes!" Patrick shrieked.

Immediately he got on the phone and proceeded to call Charles. I, on the other hand, went and got my gun and loaded it, then I walked outside beside my sister.. Snake Eyes was a character that you didn't want to be associated with, unless you had a secret death wish. I hurriedly instructed Joyce to bring my babies down the street to her home until I came by to get them later. When Snake Eyes made his way around the block again, he slowed down and then stopped in front my door. Without any pleasantries, we candidly spoke to one another. He had his gun; I had mine, too. "I want Charles," he said,

"He's not here", I answered.

"I'm looking for him", he replied.

I responded, "Whatever your feud is with Charles has nothing to do with me or my children. Please don't come back around here looking for Charles again 'because I'd die behind my babies. I'd kill behind them, too."

"I respect that, Ma," he said before speeding off. I told Patrick to tell Charles to get me and my children the hell up out of New Orleans! In less than three hours, Charles was solely responsible for me and my kids being uprooted from our home and on the road again. .

We all went to Texas by Junny and stayed in a hotel for almost two weeks. The children had a blast running around outside in the lounge area, and playing in the swimming pool. I was besides myself with all the junk and fast food they happily consumed. Nevertheless, they were truly blessed to be so young, so innocent and so carefree. I was jealous of them, but in a good way. After being cooped up in a hotel for half a month, I told Charles to get his sh*t together and fix whatever he had broken because I wanted to go home. Need-less to say, I was back in Louisiana the same day.

Charles decided to moved back in with Ms. Lynn and tried his hand at becoming a street pharmacist, all over again. This poor deci-sion landed him in jail for a second time. The only people to really suffer from this sad infraction were the little ones that grew in my womb. Charles had a remarkable record for disappointing them, but they weren't keeping score, but I was. My kids loved their daddy way more than he deserved and I knew there would someday come a time when I could no longer protect them from his cruel and thoughtless choices. For my kids, I prayed that I could over-ride his version of what success was supposed to represent. I wanted them to learn that success was measured from the inside out, not the outside in. I wish I had Charles the Teeange Dad at 15 to 17 years of age. Charles the Adult Dad was for the birds. The children and I moved from out of my parents duplex to a four bedroom apartment across town. I didn't have any furniture so I took a cue from Charles playbook and asked Michelle's boyfriend Drizzle who was already selling drugs if he'd work for me. He welcomed He welcomed the opportunity to make more cash. We made a deal as to how much I was looking to gain from his drug deals. He agree to work for me until I could pay my rent up for about three months. The money would also go towards buying household necessities we needed. He promised me it would take a couple of weeks at the most because he would be selling dope for the both of us. We agreed to certain terms and a deal was made. I felt like a hypocrite for criticizing Charles, but he and I weren't on the same playing field. There's an old wise saying that I heard the old folks say: never shit where you sleep.

It was the Wednesday before I was to make my first pickup from Drizzle when I did the dumbest thing ever; I entered a twerking contest and I didn't know how to twerk. I went to visit Carolyn at her new address and found out she lived across the street from this small club called Fabulous. I first entered the club with her to buy a sandwich from the kitchen area for her boyfriend Mike. I really liked the environment so I stayed a while and enjoyed the music. After talking with the owner for an hour or so he informed me of the dance contest happening later that evening. Being excited, I left, went home, and made a few phone calls to relatives and even Casey to join me there for a night of fun. We enjoyed ourselves immensely and frequented the lounge a total number of four times. The weekend had come and gone and I only received $300 from Drizzle so far with another promise that I would receive all the money we agreed to this coming weekend. Wednesday was upon us again and I was determined to win the dance contest at Club Fabulous even if I had to get on my head to do so. And I did. I got on my head three times and fell three times, the crowd laughed at me, but I felt like a winner and left the dance floor confident that I had won the challenge. Well, the crowd didn't agree with me, but what did they know?

It was early Mother's Day morning when the police was summoned to my door spoiling what should have been a beautiful day for me. Casey came to the house at the break of daylight beating on my door. I rose up, still dazed and answered the door. Seeing that it was Casey, I opened the door and returned to my bedroom and went back to bed. He was livid, asking me about the guy sleeping on the floor. I forgot that my old elementary schoolmate slept at my place because he was too wasted to drive home. After hearing Casey's voice, he quickly gathered his shoes and keys, then wished me a Happy Mother's Day and left. Casey stood over me, asking a lot of stupid and annoying questions as I tried to fall back sleep. When he worked my last nerve, I politely told him that in my house, I could do whatever the hell I please. I reminded him that he wasn't paying bills and he wasn't my man. Within a second, this bastard straddled me and began beating me like I was a man. When I finally broke free, I pitched my candles that were on the window sill at him as he ran out the front door and I tried chasing behind him. Realizing I couldn't catch him, I composed myself, called the police, and then his mother. I explained to her what happened between me and her son and she was shocked and she was really disappointed. We shared a woman to woman conversation about dealing with domestic abuse, but I only had one last thing to inform her of before the call came to an end. I advised her to keep her son away from me because the next time I saw him, I probably would be sending his heart to her gift wrapped in a nicely decorated box. She cried and apologized asking if I needed anything?

"I'm fine," I replied and I wished her a Happy Mother's Day before I hung up feeling anxious. A change was coming, I felt it.

SUCCESSFUL FAILURE

TWO DAYS HAD gone by and still there was no word from Drizzle about my money. I made one more attempt to reach him before I made a hasty decision. I was literally horrified to find out that he got into a gun fight with someone whom he searched out for revenge and was killed. I was stumped on how I was going to take care of my babies, but God always made a way out of no way. I had the same $300 dollars Drizzle gave me almost three weeks ago. I needed to get away and think about what I was going to do about my finances, so I asked my cousin Brent to stay over with the kids until my return. I hugged my babies and left as soon as possible because I didn't want them to see me crying and upset. I went uptown, near my mama's part of town and checked into the neighborhood motel called the Rochambeau and got a room. I had no intentions of being there no more than one night, but Casey convinced me otherwise. He had a relative working there and she informed him that I had checked in for the night. When he showed up I was to broken down to argue or to be irritated by his presence. After he apologized for the second act of causing me bodily harm, I relayed to him the current status of the situation pertaining to my state of affairs. He told me to give him the $300 and he would triple it so I wouldn't lose the house and that he was starting a new job. As a friend, he said he would help me with the utilities until I could get a decent job. I was very leery when it came to Casey's promises, but I had nothing to lose. So, stupidly, I trusted him.

I stayed in the motel for an entire week without notifying anyone of my where about. I was truly a lost soul until I remembered the vow I made to God about never running away from home again. When I came back to myself, I called Casey and told him I was ready to check out of the hotel and he said he'd be right there with my money. Well, that turned out to be a fat lie. The $300 that he promised he would triple for me was paying for the hotel room I had been in for seven days. When I learned this shit, I was distraught and outraged at how deceitful Casey could be. One minute he was a very good friend, the next he was Charles to the third power. As I left the hotel and headed back home, I tried not to think about the negative situation that I was in. Instead, I concentrated on the positive, which at the moment only gave me a hint of a smile. When I reached my babies, they were truly glad to see me and gave me huge hugs and kisses as their evidence. When I entered the kitchen, I apologized to Brent for my unforeseen disappearing act and asked if anyone else were concerned with my where a bouts? Brent simply stated that no one called or had been by. The only phone call was from Charles. "Charles, huh?" I sighed, I didn't bother to ask what the conversation was about. I just wanted to stop thinking for just a few moments. To have a little peace of mind temporarily wasn't too much to ask for?

Charles was released from jail the same day I got my eviction notice. When the kids saw him, they were delighted and overjoyed. I felt indifferent. After tiring the kids out and making them take a nap, Charles came over to my bed and kissed me ever so lightly on the forehead. He told me the details of how he managed to not go insane being away from his family and that we were all that he thought about. After talking about our problems out in the open, we came to an understanding that as a couple we didn't have a conclusive answer on how we should proceed in our marriage. I suggested that in order to have any type of bond, we needed to become friends again. We agreed to give it a try.

About two days after Charles had moved back in with me and the kids, we began receiving late night phone-calls. Each night after Charles answered the calls, he would get dressed and leave for a few hours, then return. On the fifth night, I put the phone on my side of the bed when Charles fell asleep, so I could answer it. Like clockwork, the call came at about 2:30am. I picked up the receiver and said hello. The voice on the other line was familiar, but I didn't catch it right away.

"May I speak to Charles, may I speak to Charles?" She stuttered.

"Shelia? Is this Shelia?" I asked again.

This time she responded with a yes. "What do you want with Charles?" I asked.

"Nita I need him 'cause I messed up," she stated.

I told her OK and I gave Charles the phone. When Charles got up to get dressed, I was up getting dressed too, but we never left the house that night or any night not for Shelia.

Being that Charles and I concluded that being friends was in our best interest for our kids, I made a small suggestion to him as a friend to go to Club Fabulous to see the ladies dance and gyrate for the men. He eagerly agreed to go. The following night while Charles was out with his brother and their friends, Carolyn came by the house and told me there was something important she had to show me. My cousin Brent and the children were sound asleep, so I had no reason not to satisfy my curiosity. First we went to her house across the street from Club Fabulous where I shockingly discovered my mama had moved into the empty apartment on the opposite side of her. My visit wasn't nothing special with my family so I asked Carolyn if this was the important thing she had to reveal to me.

"I'm about to show you, Nita but I had to cash my check first to buy food from the kitchen in the club. We can go now. Come on," she teased, I had to admit I was really curious now.

When we went into the club, it was full to capacity. There were people everywhere in this small establishment. Carolyn and I fought our way through the crowd to get to the kitchen. Because I came with her free and willingly, Carolyn decided to treat me to a late night dinner, too. While we were waiting on the food to be prepared, she began to explain to me why she came to retrieve me. She said my sister

Sheila came and borrowed a bathing suit to dance in tonight. And at that moment, Carolyn guided my head to the dance floor where Charles was seated. What I saw made me want to puke. Sheila was laid out on the floor in front of Charles, doing things that a female should reserve only for her significant other. But never-the-less, she was in front of a packed crowd of about 250-300 perverts and her focus was solely on my spouse. When Charles spotted me staring at them in disbelief, he got up and walked out the club with Sheila chasing after him. After the food was prepared and ready for pick-up, I requested that Carolyn bring me back home; I had enough revelation for one night. Charles didn't come back to the house that night. I could only imagine what he thought I could or would do if he did.

Ms. Lynn and Charles came by the house a few days later to get me and the kids. I was guessing that Charles spoke to her about my living situation. I was exhausted with beating myself up on what I could have done differently. We were riding around in a very nice black Buick Skylark. I can't exactly remember the year of the car, but it was really nice. I was wondering where and how did Charles purchase this car. He was shifting the car gears like it gave him more pleasure than a woman. We dropped the kids off with their aunts and uncles, then headed on a search to find Ms. Lynn a home to purchase. I soon found out Ms. Lynn had come into a nice sum of money and was in search of becoming a home owner.

Well it didn't take us long to find her a special piece of property. This particular piece of land had two homes for the price of one. They both were a beauty and together, they were a steal. Ms. Lynn loved her estate which was a large 3 three bedroom apartment building that was beautifully modified into a two family living quarters with a storage area /driveway. A renovated cottage was behind the main estate. We moved into the new places within a couple of days and I welcomed the change of scenery. The stability for my children and the love they had from their family. I envisioned that the beauty and comfort the cottage exuded would be beneficial to me with my hope of reconnecting to Jesus. Things were going well as could be expected with Charles and I, despite the incidents prior to moving back in with each other in what appeared to be on a more permanent basis. In the back of my mind, I was strategically planning a new way to deal with that familiar inferno when it should arise to swallow me whole.

Charles and I were getting ready for bed when we got an urgent call from my mama to come see her. She wouldn't give us any details over the phone pertaining to her problem, causing me and Charles to really wonder why the need for all the urgency. The ride took almost twenty minutes and sleep was beginning to over shadow our desire to come to my mama's aide. When we pulled up to the door of my mother's new residence, my siblings were all gathered outside on the porch enthralled in laughter, causing me to really speculate about what kind of emergency warranted me and my spouse to cast our sleep aside. Nobody seemed worried or like there was a sense of urgency at all. When we walked into my mama's bedroom, she was lying in bed with a baby that I didn't recognized. She asked me and Charles to sit down as she began to tell us the tale of why we were summoned. A few nights ago, she went to the emergency room for a terrible migraine headache. While she was with the doctor, Shelia who had accompanied her was out in the waiting area, had struck up a conversation with a homeless woman. The woman had a baby girl named Breanne Hathaway that was a couple of days old and was a crack baby. After feeling comfortable with Shelia, the woman asked her to hold the baby while she attended the restroom, but the lady never came back. End of story. I guess this is where Charles and I came in, but I wasn't sure what our role was supposed to be yet. So, reluctantly, I asked my mother why she called us. She said the baby needed food and pampers and she didn't know what to do; therefore she called us. The night ended with Charles and I driving back home with a new baby and a whole lot of unanswered questions. The main question being what in the hell did we just do?

For three days we tried feeding her, keeping her diapers dry, rocking her, driving around with her, but nothing seemed to quiet this baby. It wasn't until Michelle came to the cottage and retrieved her that we were finally able to get a bit of rest. After Michelle had the child with her a couple of days, we went to make sure we weren't putting her in an uncomfortable and compromising position in caring for this beautiful innocent infant. As we sat with Michelle and the baby I asked her what she did to calm Breanne to help her sleep. Michelle said she simply rub her in the middle of her spine while slowly rocking her. This helped to soothe the drug cravings the baby was experiencing. That broke my heart. While I was chatting it up with Michelle, Charles went to the cottage to check up on our children only to return to informed me that my mama had called, wanting us to come back to see her and to bring the baby, too. When we made it over to mama's place, my siblings were all huddled up outside on the sidewalk awaiting our arrival like we were the enemy. When we got out of the car and headed up the steps toward the entrance of the house we could smell the barbecue chicken mama had baked hours earlier. Thinking I was called over for a meal, I immediately made my way to the kitchen thinking the food would be out and awaiting our presence, but I was wrong.

"OK mama, we are here. So what's the deal?" I asked walking into her bedroom. Before mama could answer me, Shelia walked through the door with the troop following behind her in a rage about me having Breanne without her given consent. I thought the shit was hilarious. I decided to stay cool and not feed into the hype that my sister was trying to build this situation into and quietly gave my mama all the things pertaining to the child that *Charles and I* bought and we left the premises. When we made it back to the house without the baby, Michelle was deeply disappointed and the kids were sadden also. From that day on, Charles and I made an agreement that my mother and her children's grievances weren't mine, but hers to bear, especially if it involved Shelia.

A few weeks passed and Charles had begun working at yet another Circle K. This time, though, it was a mini mart that didn't sell any gasoline. I was leery and weary of Circle K's with or without the gas. The evening Charles came home from his first initial day back at work, we got into a huge argument. I was in the process of cooking rice when Charles came stomping through the door angry and upset about something he considered serious, but I had no idea what it was. I walked over and sweet-talked him into telling me the problem hoping I could make him feel better. He somehow found out Pamela was pregnant and was upset because she denied that the baby belonged to him. This clown just never ceased to amaze me. The dispute got so heated that Charles grabbed me by my throat once more and slammed me into the wall before disappearing upstairs to attend to a crying Charlita who apparently was awakened and scared by his actions. I was so shaken up by the assault that I dropped the pot of hot boiling water all over my arm as I attempted to strain the rice into the colander. Hearing me scream brought Charles to my side as I ran into the bathroom running cold water on the burning sensation flowing down my right arm to my wrist. Realizing this wasn't helping the situation, he took me to the Emergency room, which was a better decision. Four hours later, I was bandaged up and sent home with a couple of prescriptions for painkillers and two different types of burn creams. He apologized a hundred times blaming himself for the accident. All I wanted to do was forget the incident and get some sleep and I advised Charles to do the same.

Charles had been doing so well on his job. He was promoted to a managerial position at a new location several blocks away within a couple of months. The old routine was starting to settle in when he was beginning to be away from home more and more. The day he brought work home with him was the day when I had to bring that idea that I had reserved in the back of my mind about leaving Charles out to the fore front and into reality. We were doing the dishes together, something that almost never happens, when he begins to tell me about one of his female employees named Bev. Shocked by the simple first name I asked was her last name Jones. He answered yes, amusingly.

"I went to school with her," I carelessly stated. This only opened the door for him to tell me of all the subtle hints of affection she displayed to assure him of her interest in him. Indeed, Charles had been on the prowl again and he found his next victim. This time around, it was my determination to be better prepared to handle the chaos that was sure to disrupt the lives of my four precious faces.

The next day, my boys were out in the yard swinging on the archway between the two properties with their cousins when they accidentally broke the wall of the archway and made an astonishing discovery. Inside of the wall was money from the era of the early Spanish settlers of the 1700's. The children instantly ran inside to their grandmother house ecstatic and overjoyed with their findings. They thought it was Mardi Gras Doubloons. When I learned of their discovery. I thanked God for the small blessing because I knew this was his way of opening the door for me to leave and get away from Charles for good. Ms. Lynn, however wouldn't hear of sharing any of the Spanish coins with me. Yet and still, I didn't feel defeated.

Sunshine came to the cottage a few days later and confided in me that she thought her mama was being unfair and promised to help me get some of the money when her family were all away from the house around the 1st of the month. Like promised, Sunshine came through and told me of her mama's hidden spot for the coins and I got as many as I could and went to rare coin collector in the French Quarters and sold them all for about $3000. I gave Sunshine $350 and held onto the remainder of the money for when mad day came; and believe me, it was coming.

I was bored one night while Charles was at work. I decided to go visit him on his job, so I got dressed, left the house and headed his way. When I made it to the mini store, Charles was not there. In fact, the store was open, but completely unattended. After waiting out front for about thirty minutes, I decide to walk around toward the back when I heard familiar voices; it was Charles and Bev having sex in the storeroom. I ran out the store in a blind rage and called Casey from the first pay-phone I saw.

It was in the wee hours of morning when I returned home and Charles was up waiting for me. He had the audacity to be angry and outraged as he demanded answers on where I had been. I was indignant and I disrespectfully told him to kiss my ass. He grabbed me around the collar and became more infuriated when he noticed my shirt was on backwards.

"So, this what we doing now?" He asked through gritted teeth.

When I didn't respond he threw me down to the floor, I walked out the front door to keep from waking the kids, but he stayed in pursuit. Within seconds we were in front of his mother's property where he was making a spectacle out of me. Humiliated, I left and walked to the nearest pay- phone again, but this time I called and waited for the police. When they came, I was escorted back to the house and got my belongings; the only things I wanted and took were my children. I'd never been so happy to be in the back of a squad car.

For a month straight, I had a consistent dream about chaos in my marriage and being in harm's way since receiving the money from the coins. The dream was so intense that I made a conscious choice a couple of days prior to the night of the incident to rent an apartment for me and the children. The weird thing about the place I rented was the fact that it was Larry's very first place that he ever had on his own.

I was happy with my quaint one bedroom apartment. I didn't have any furniture or a refrigerator yet, but I had all the essentials we needed such as soap, towels, sheets, etc. I also bought my boys their school uniforms, sneakers and school supplies. It was now 1992 and I was hoping that Charlita would get into pre-kindergarten, but that was just wishful thinking because I knew she was too smart. Still, I sat aside a personal day to bring her school shopping. I went to visit Theresa's on the boys first day of school and she took me to meet one of her older gentlemen friends who hired me as a barmaid for 6 days out of the week. I was to start in two weeks. That would be enough time for me to get my business situated and make sure my children were attended to properly in my absence. I was quickly gaining renewing momentum in reconnecting to Jesus and it gave me an unspeakable joy.

On the boys third day of class, I decided to bring my anxious little girl to the mall to shop for school. She was so thrilled and full of life at the very thought of being in the same building as her brothers that even the downpour of rain we got caught in didn't damper her spirits. Once inside the mall, I let her choose her own personal cartoon character for her school supplies which included the engraving of her name. With no surprise to me, she chose Hello Kitty for everything. I'm talking umbrella, rain-boots, pencils, tablets, crayons, pencil case, raincoat, scissors, glue… everything! If they made it for school, she owned it. I never saw a little girl happier than mine. For this reason, I could never hate Charles because he gave me her and my beautiful boys.

It was Monday and also Charlita's testing day. She was nervous. Her three fabulous brothers gave her encouragement which seemed to help her regain her composure before they headed off to school. My baby was the third child scheduled to be tested that morning so we were there a little early. It was hard to keep her busy. Not because she was an unruly child, but due to her heightened interest in learning new things. To occupy her time, I allowed her to help me fill out her school application and enrollment forms. We were just finishing up when the teacher advised me that the time had arrived for my interview. It was during this time that my baby went over to the activity table in the class where the puzzles were nicely put together and began dismantling them. The teacher momentarily looked up and glanced Charlita's way. The teacher quickly became aggravated and displeased. She asked her through clinched teeth to not take the puzzles apart because she would not have the time to re-assemble them. Feeling somewhat offended, I shared with her that if my baby took them apart, she could put them back together. The teacher implied that it took the students to the end of the school year to accomplish such a task. I had to show this woman better than I could tell her, so I told Charlita to put the puzzles back together. My daughter was a show off, she put the four different fifty piece puzzles she took apart back together again, upside down and walked over to the table where the teacher and I were seated and asked were there any other puzzles that were harder. The teacher responded by saying she'd be in touch with me soon and promptly dismissed us. We never did get a call back. I did however, get a letter from the school stating that Charlita wouldn't be admitted to the Pre-K program because she was too advance and would intimidate the other students. My little girl was disappointed, but not for long. She simply asked if she could try again the following year. I nodded, and she wrapped her tiny arms around me as I kissed her face. Theresa came to the apartment that evening to inform me that Mr. Mack, her friend, was opening the bar earlier than expected and needed me to work a couple hours later on that night and wanted to know if I was available. I told her to send word to him that it wouldn't be a problem and that I would be there at 8pm, sharp. Since moving into the neighborhood, I had developed a good relationship with two mothers on the block, Zane and Leslie. I told them about my job and they both agreed to look out and look in on my kids while I was at work. I helped my kids with their homework, fed them, made sure they had their bible lesson and baths all before I left for work at 7:30pm. When I returned home about 12:30am, Zane was sitting on her stoop waiting up for me.

"How was your first night, Anita?" she asked me.

"Girl, not too bad!" I announced feeling happy about having a job. "How were my babies?" I asked. "You got good kids, Nita. They went to bed right at 8 just like you said they would," she proclaimed.

"Thank you so much, Zane! I owe you one, girl! Thanks again, good night," I sounded off as I got up and walked across the street toward my home.

"No problem, Anita. Good night." she yelled back before heading inside, herself.

When I turned the key to the door, there was Charlita waiting up for me, demanding cookies at almost 1:00 am. I couldn't refuse her, so I put her shoes on and we strolled to the liquor store a few blocks away. While we were walking, my little chatter box told me everything that happened since I left her company. Once we made it to the store, I noticed it was full of all kinds of night creeps. I went into over-protective mode when an older man that I knew was harmless, made a comment on how pretty my little girl was, but I was caught off guard by the stranger behind me that made the comment that her mother was also beautiful. Right away I walked up to the window and made my purchases and speedily walked home as fast as I could with my baby in tow. When I was about to turn the key and enter into my house, I was startled by a man's voice coming from behind me; it was the guy that made the comment about me being beautiful. I set Charlita inside the apartment on the floor and told her to eat her snacks, and that I wasn't going far. Then, I ushered the man away from my door and asked him what he wanted?

"I just want to talk," he insisted.

As we sat on the steps to the barbershop which was literally next door to my apartment, I told him I couldn't invite him into my place because I didn't have any furniture for him to sit on. He wanted to know why? This dude just didn't let up. I took a deep sigh and began telling him about my fight with Charles and how I wind up here at this particular place and point in my life. He told me his name, which I didn't remember, but said he could help me and if I trusted him, he promised not to disappoint me. I said alright and bid him good night, not expecting to see this man again. But God was on a mission to reassure me he was the Almighty and there was nothing that He couldn't do. As I was making my pallet on the floor to go to sleep I was interrupted by a knock on the door. Wondering who it could be, I hurried to the door and carefully opened it to the stranger that left me only a short time earlier. He returned with so much furniture, my apartment wasn't big enough to receive it all. As the men loaded up my house, I thanked him and apologized for being so rude toward him. He said that my attitude was the driving force of why he returned and it proved to him I was no ordinary woman. His compliment made my heart smile. When the stranger and his compadres left, I made up the beds and tucked my kids in the proper way, before heading to the bathroom to shower. While lathering, I couldn't help but break down into to tears over the miraculous occurrences that were over taking my life. I was more grateful to God beyond what mere words could ever express.

Well the following day, I got a much unexpected surprise. The kind stranger came back again to check on me and the children. While we were in the beginning stage of our conversation, Charles shows up with his hand extended and introduces himself as my well to do husband. His arrogant demeanor caused my guardian angel to become a bit uncomfortable and he nervously excused himself and went on his way. My heart sunk to the pit of my stomach as I watched him leave. Charles followed me into the apartment barking at me about coming back to the cottage and him missing his daughter. I was tired and needed to cook. On top of that, I needed to rest for work later on that night. I didn't have time or wanted to be bothered with Charles and his tantrums. He became more irate upon noticing I was not tuning into his childish rambling. In retaliation, he tried to grab Charlita away from me while I was combing her hair. When he realized I was not going to let her go, he picked up one of her sneakers and threw it at me, hitting me in my right temple, barely missing my eye. After this brief act of violence, he got in his car and left. It took all the energy I had left to console the fears of my scared little girl. By the time the boys were home from school, I was drained and needed a nap. My sons had such a beautiful love and an unbreakable bond with their sister that gave me a sense of peace that others could never really understand. I informed CJ that dinner was on the stove and that they all could go out and play once their homework was done. I reminded them to make sure they kept an eye on Charlita. He nodded in my direction and before I knew it, I was sound asleep.

Charles came by a few days later with a peace offering. He brought me a bowl of gumbo that he made personally for the first time ever. I didn't have time to eat it right away. I had to get to work. It was the weekend and the tips were bound to be good that night. He offered to give me a ride to work, but I declined. I was not going to give in to him or allow him to control any other aspect of my life. If he would have come by with some type of monetary assistance for the kids, then maybe we could've talked.

While attending the bar that night, I met a lot of new faces as they mixed in with the regulars. Some were married couples while others were single or in bad relationships. The kitchen was open and the aromas from the foods cooking were overwhelming and infectious. The bar was in full affect that night. Theresa and I stayed a while after the bar closed and had a few casual drinks, catching up on family and current events; in other words, we were shamelessly gossiping. About 3:00am, we went our separate ways and I looked forward to what the day was to bring. Before I went to bed, I wanted to know what Charles gumbo tasted like.

It was payday and I was over eager to be rewarded for my long hours and challenging work. This would be my first real paycheck, something that represented my true independence and my commitment to establish myself as a victor, not a victim, a status that has towered over me for quite some time. Since it had been a while and I was in the neighborhood, I decided to stop by my grandmother's place. When I walked through the front door, she and my Aunt Rose gave me a warm and loving greeting. I shared with them how good my kids were doing and told them all about my job and they gave me information on other family members and what they considered to be newsworthy. As I was about to leave, Aunt Rose took me by the hand and asked me how I was feeling? I explained to her that I probably had a cold or the flu due to the late nights I walked home from work and that lack of sleep was also an ongoing problem. She advised me that I was not looking so well, that my skin looked pale and the appearance of my eyes were yellowish. She endearingly stated I needed to go to the doctor and soon. I told her I would and I left feeling a little worried, but shrugged it off.

The weeks were coming and going and I was becoming thinner with a low lack of energy. Business at the bar was beginning to slow down and I was coming home a lot earlier now. On one early evening and I was resting in bed when I felt the surge of life leaving me. Immediately, my eyes flew open and there was a female black cat standing in my chest in an attack stance with our noses inches away from each other. She was literally sucking my life out of me. With the little life I had left, I called on the name of Jesus. The cat hissed at me and leaps out the window the same way she came in. When I sat up in the bed and looked out the window, I could swear there were at least a hundred cats gathered outside near my opening. I slammed the window down and then got on my knees to pray. Later on that day, while I was trying to rest, my sister Shelia came by claiming to have a present for me. I didn't want her gift or her company, but she was there and I couldn't put up much of a fight any way; I was so tired. When I sat up in bed again, she brought a crack-headed stranger into my apartment. She was genuinely surprised that I didn't recognize who he was. Realizing I was not in the mood for playing guessing games, she declared that he was my prom date from junior high school. After gazing over his presence and remembering how he embarrassed me on my prom night by abandoning me and flirting with every single girl who attended prom that evening, I found my voice and told both of these addicts to promptly get the hell out of my house. Just when I thought things were going to be better, that sleep and I would be reacquainted for a couple of hours, I received more visitors. This time it was my mother and she also had a surprise guest tagging alongside her. It was her old boyfriend from my childhood. As she entered my apartment with this man, I sat in my bed frozen, as if I was a glass artifact that was designed not born. I stared at him relentlessly and he smiled back at me challenging me to say something, anything. But I couldn't. I felt like that terrified little girl he abused and molested. He knew that there was nothing I could do or say that would cause him to pay for his crimes or cause my mama to turn against him, and he was right. At that moment, the fellow who assisted me home from work the night before came by to check on me. When he walked into the apartment he could feel the tension and it confused him. Minutes later, Casey walked through the door with a dozen and a half of beautiful red roses and notices the eeriness in the room. He asked the young man to come back at a later time, then he beckoned my mother and the stranger outside for a brief word or two. Minutes later, he returned into the apartment, alone. When he sat next to me, I crumble into a massive mess as my tears flowed like the Nile River. I was releasing years of pinned up shame and dirtiness and the guilt of being born a female. Casey was there to shield me from my past disgrace once again and I sincerely was relieved.

A couple more weeks went by and the bar wasn't doing well at all. My days were cut down from 6 to 3 a week. I was coming home from picking up my check when I fainted during my walk back home. I was assisted by my neighbor Zane and her son Philip who just so happen to see me while on their way to the grocery store. Once I was home, Zane was adamant about me seeing a doctor. She went and checked the kids out of school early and called the ambulance to bring me to Mercy Hospital. I didn't put up a fuss because I knew she had my best interest at heart and she was a very good friend.

I went to the emergency room and they ran a plethora of test and diagnosed me with the flu. The doctor gave me a prescription for antibiotics and instructed me to drink plenty of fluids along with bed rest. Even though this was my diagnosis, I was not comfortable with the thought that this was my true problem, but how can you argue with the doctors and their test results. I was discharged and sent home feeling no better than before the visit.

It was a couple of weeks later when I couldn't fight what I was feeling no longer. My energy was nearly depleted. I barely had enough strength to stay awake with my children. I had been having bible lessons with them and I'd end it by asking them a very pertinent question that made a world of a difference to me, "What good can you say about your mama?" My babies didn't have an answer at that time. They didn't realize it made a difference to me because it decided whether or not I wanted to live or die. We were watching videos on our 19inch black and white TV when I saw the Angel of death come down and kiss me. I could hear my kids scream my name, but I was paralyzed, in a spiritual trance and couldn't answer them. I had a meeting with Jesus.

I had apparently went into a coma and the doctors called my family together and compassionately advised them of the seriousness of my condition. As I was regaining consciousness, my mom, Junny, along with a few other family members who had visited me were leaving, but their sitting next to the bed and holding my hand although he was asleep was Casey. When I had gain full conscious, he was so enthralled with the fact that I was awake, he started to cry. I was so touched to have someone at my side through this trying time, I started to cry to because I died and conversed with God for three days and I also danced with devil. There was no one I could share this with without coming off as crazy, so I just kept it to myself. I stayed in the hospital approximately three and a half to four weeks. I didn't have any visitors other than Casey, who encouraged me daily that my kids were depending on me to get better. Upon my discharge from the hospital, a social worker arranged for me to have transportation to get home safely. When I got to my residence all my things were discarded on the sidewalk like common trash. I was absolutely devastated. Realizing this wasn't my home any more, I had the taxi driver bring me to Theresa's house not too far away. After arriving there, Charles drove up unexpectedly with my daughter, relieving me of a heavy weight that was on my shoulders; he let me know the boys were safe with his mom and they would be back with me before Monday for school. By Sunday night, I was at Theresa's place, regretting the fact that I was there in the first place because she made it perfectly clear that me and my children were a nuisance. But I had nowhere else to go. Then, Casey came to visit me. When he came to the house, I was shocked and happy to see him; I never thanked him for being there for me during such a horrific ordeal. He asked me did I have a clue on how the poison got into my system. I told him I didn't get sick until I ate Charles's gumbo and I was more than sure he could have tried to kill me. What made this attempt any different than the others? He said he came by because he had a surprise for me and the kids. Collectively, we all came together and took a short stroll to a house that were only a few blocks away. Thinking we were visiting one of his family members, I became a little frustrated because I wasn't feeling my best. When he opened the door to the house, we instantly recognized that the one bedroom home was furnished with us in mind. We were thrilled and extremely excited to be in our own place again. Casey really came through this time. Was he the knight in shining armor that Eric spoke of? My heart said no, but my mind said yes.

Settling into the new place with Casey came with ease since we tried it prematurely before. Now that he had a stable job, I was sure things were going to be a whole lot different this time around especially, since he took the initiative to become the man of the house by providing the house. The only thing we were lacking in the house was a refrigerator which didn't last for too long because Charles gave us the one from the cottage. Any way he felt like I needed him, satisfied his appetite for control over me. The fact that Casey allowed Charles into our home to take care of a need in our home made me feel so unsafe and bothered. I never looked at Casey the same after this incident. I became a nervous wreck knowing that I had to depend on Casey to save me against the big bad wolf. My health declined again and I went back into the hospital after being home for 8 days. I was hospitalized for two more weeks.

When I was released, I promised myself I would manage my anger much better and become content with my life for the moment because my kids couldn't afford for me to keep disappearing on them. Although I should have stayed in bed, once I was back home, I begged Casey to bring me to get my kids a Christmas tree. While we were out getting this tree, Charles apparently made his way to our home and made quite a disturbance that caused the neighbors across the street to become involved in chasing him away. This news infuriated me and Casey's calm attitude about it didn't help make me feel any better.

The Thanksgiving holidays were upon us and the children were going over to Ms. Lynn's home to enjoy the weekend after turkey day. I was too ill to cook, but pleasantly surprised when Casey's mom prepared an entire dinner for me and my family. I was so blessed and fortunate. I had plenty to be so grateful and thankful for. When my children returned from their grandma's, I was not as blissful as I normally would be. Something about my children was off, I just didn't know what. I had been having dreams of chaos with my estranged ex and my dreams were always sure to come true.

In the meantime, the children were enjoying movies we rented from blockbusters when I noticed that all three of my boys were sitting on their hands. When I asked what happened, I was told that their daddy whipped them with a board across their bottoms for misbehaving. When I asked to see the results of the whipping, I became hysterical, realizing my sons butts must had been beaten raw and bloody. I was appalled and terrified at what I might do. I immediately called Casey into the room and showed him my sons and he was in utter dismay, too. He did his best to soothe my madness, He also went to call the police. When the police came out, they took me and the kids down to police headquarters and filed a formal complaint, took pictures, promised they would be in touch with a hearing date and then they brought us back home.

Once I put my children to bed, I went across the street to the pay phone and called Charles, something I know I shouldn't have done, but I was pissed. He accused me of lying about the bruising on the boys, stating they were just as discrepant as the claims that I made on behalf of Charlita against Darren (Michelle's degenerate boyfriend) for indecently touching and molesting her almost a month ago. The resentment that swelled in me was only a centimeter from bursting my heart as I remembered my young daughter's outcry while having this grown woman examination to see if indeed she had been violated. The examination definitely confirmed that she was molested, but wasn't penetrated. He talked real brave on the other end of the phone, but I promised Charles that God always kept score. Afterwards, I slammed the receiver on the hook and went home angrier than before.

It was a pleasing revelation to know my sister Joyce had moved around the corner from me. I really missed my sister and what we used to be before she married my old high school friend, Ray. I knew he was no good for her and because of this we, inevitably drifted apart. When I couldn't get any relief from my pain from the poison in my system, I would often borrow money from her to buy Nyquil so that I could have something to help me cope with my pain and put me to sleep because my prescriptions, alone, didn't work. It also felt good to have a family member frequent my house as much as I frequented hers. Besides, I was extremely happy to visit with my sister because she had custody of Breanne, who was getting so big.

I went over to Ms. Lynn to let her see the boys for a short while, when she gave me some strange news. Charles and Bev were in love. I thought it was so sweet, but it turned out that Bev was a married woman. Imagine that. Bev and her husband got into a serious fight the night before pertaining to Charles. The argument led to him beating her up, atrociously. She had walked to Ms. Lynn's house, battered and bruised. She told Ms. Lynn and Charles what happened. Charles, being drunk and stupid, went to this Bev's house to confront her husband about beating her up. Needless to say, not only was Charles arrested and in jail, but he also had a very high bond. Nobody was able to come up with the money to bail him out, either. Out of the whole ordeal, the only things that was disturbing to me was Ms. Lynn's sympathy for Bev and the fact that she believed Bev could make her son's life better. I was trying to comprehend her logic. Her son was in jail over *someone else's* wife. I was so glad when my sons visit with her was over. Being there bought back a memory so painful, it almost caused me to have a mental breakdown right at that moment. The straw that broke the camel's back for me and Charles was when we scheduled a meeting at the cottage a while back to talk about the kids and where we were in our lives, pertaining to our children. We sat and talk and laughed about old times for a while. Then, we shared things that we never wanted to talk about again, but it was therapeutic. One of the things we talked about was our sex life, or the lack thereof. We both had to admit that that played a huge role in our destructed relationship because even though I had four kids, I was inept as a lover. Charles asked me to give him one more chance to see if we ever were truly making love; if he couldn't make me feel the love, he would let me go. I obliged and we began having sex to music, which always made it easier for me whenever I was intimate with him because I always go to a different place in my mind to alleviate the pain. During the act, the song Lately by Jodeci came on and he stopped midway through the song and broke down as he sobbed and confessed his love for me. Almost simultaneously, there was a knock on the cottage door. We both were naked and confused on whether or not to even answer the door, but the knocker was persistent. Charles decided to wrap himself in one of the sheets and went downstairs to see what was urgent. I laid there waiting to hear voices, but couldn't hear a pin drop. After laying there for about the first twenty minutes, tears flowed down my cheeks; I felt so used and dirty. The twenty minutes turned into an hour, then an hour turned in to almost two hours before he returned. He didn't know what to say, he knew there was nothing to say. He understood that this would never happened again and that he hurt me a thousand times in a thousand ways, but this hurt was damn near unforgivable. I had just confided in him that I recognized my shortcomings in this marriage and accepted my failures and faults, but to have Bev, his other woman, take up his time after sexually bonding with me was degrading and downright heinous. I got dressed and promised never to forget that night; it made me realize I was stronger than I could ever have imagined.

CJ had started acting out, mainly because he missed his daddy. He didn't want to be around me so much so, that Joyce allowed him to live with her around the corner. When she brought Breanne with her to visit, she would bring CJ, too. CJ really didn't want to live with his Aunt Joyce, but my son had too much pride to apologize for his behavior so he could return home. Dallas came by and drop the kids off a big fluffy white rabbit. They still hadn't gotten over me accidentally killing their first rabbit, Fluffy. That became even more evident because they keep the pet away from me. It hurt my feelings, but I understood. Casey and I went out and bought the kids gifts to put under the Christmas tree we purchased the week before. I bought the children new shoes and outfits to look nice for the holiday so they could enjoy Christmas day with thanksgiving in their heart and realize how good GOD had been to them. My kids didn't really ask for much; I knew that they were going to love their gifts.

My joy from getting the kids gift quickly dissipated when I tried using my ATM card, and it didn't work. The machine was out of paper, so I couldn't get my balance. Casey finally confessed to me that our bank account had over-draft fees of at least $385. When we made it to the bank, I was very honest with him about how I felt about the ordeal.

I looked at my adultery partner and said with a great big smile, "Everything is going to be alright, Casey. Someday, and someday soon, I'm going to leave you".

He responded with a smile, "That'll never happen".

"Time, Boo. It's all about timing," I replied then planted a light kiss across his lips before we went to the next available teller. We paid the fees owed, retrieved our last $400 and closed the account.

I had nothing better to do then to meet up with Theresa and get into something I had no business doing. I helped her cash checks that belonged to her neighbor, who was a drug addict. Theresa and I split the money 50/50. We chucked it up as us deserving it more than her drug addicted neighbor did because she was dope fiend and was going to use the funds for drugs anyway. At the end of the day, I still was not proud of what we did, but I kept the money and put it toward a new residence for the New Year.

It was Christmas Eve and we were cooking and wrapping Christmas gifts when I got a knock at the door. Since Casey was saddled down with wrapping gifts, I stepped over him to answer the door and was dumbfounded to see a sheriff deputy asking for Anita Duke.

"I'm Anita Duke." I said shakily.

"You've been served," he announced, after which he placed a

brown envelope in my hand. "Merry Christmas to you Ma'am," he stated as he departed. I closed the door and stood staring back and forth at Casey and the envelope. He beckoned me to open it and I hesitantly obeyed. When I read its contents, I broke out in an uncontrollable laugh that gave me a headache. Casey was baffled and asked what was funny. Still laughing, I handed the papers over to him. It was a divorce decree hand written by Charles Duke, himself. He was divorcing me on the grounds of irreconcilable differences and I had thirty days to contest it or the divorce would be finalized. By far, this was the best Christmas present I could have ever received from Charles!

THE NOUN OF MY NOW

CHARLES GOT OUT of jail and came to my house with Bev to pick up Charlita. I didn't answer the door when he came and I had no idea he brought Bev with him. Had I known, it wouldn't have been a quiet morning on my block. Charlita showed no reaction to seeing him nor cared about going off with him, either. I gather it would have been quite different with the boys. About three months later, Charles came by asking to speak to me. I half-heartedly obliged because he seemed really desperate and anxious. He had the appearance of the Charles I knew when we were 15 years old. He took me to Irving's house so we could have a quiet place to converse. He began to apologize. Then he spoke about a woman named Star, whom he had known and had a crush on since high school. He also stated how she reminded him of me. He said he wanted me to meet her because he think he was falling in love with her. I listened to him attentively and told him I'd meet her and I wished him all the luck in the world. After that, he brought me back home. Charles and Star came over the following day to meet my kids and she seemed very nice. She immediately fell in love with Charlita. God is so funny because right after I met Star, I unfortunately went into the hospital to have surgery and she and Charles took care of the kids. I was glad she was with Charles because it gave me a peace of mind. When I came home from the hospital, Casey was being very supportive. He tried to boost my morale because I had suffered severe hair lost. I found out in the hospital that I had cervical cancer and they immediately began my Chemo treatment. Casey cut off my hair to make it even. I felt so ugly and exposed, but he helped me put on my makeup and then he made me look in the mirror at myself to see how beautiful I looked. I looked real hard, too, but didn't see it. Casey had his cousin come over later that evening with a trunk full of clothes and they created me a personal wardrobe. I was so overwhelmed. I knew Casey loved me, but there were so many things we needed to fix to be a better couple. I thought that if I Was his wife, we'd be able to fix it. Since I was divorced, he was indifferent to the subject of marriage whenever I brought it up. I always knew he wouldn't really marry me, but he promised otherwise.

The time came for us to move into a bigger place, so we rented a two bedroom home uptown that was very nice and quaint. I loved the location of the house because we lived near a lot of important places. We were there three months and Casey messed up his check again. I had no idea how, but I didn't fret. My cousin Rachel who lived really close by told me about a temporary job employment service she worked for. The company was looking to hire new people every day.

"I'll do it. I just need you to come get me when you get ready to go to the job site," I responded.

"Will do, Cousin. Be ready at 4:30pm," Rachel stated, before she left.

The next day, when Casey made it home from work, I informed him of the eviction notice that came and he swore it was a mistake.

I told him, "It's okay. Everything is going to be alright. I'm leaving you," I smirked. He grabbed me by throat and said that that'll never happen. Then, he let me go. I put my hand to my throat and gently rubbed the area where he left his finger indention. I informed Casey that putting his hands on me would cause his mother to bury a child, and I warned him to never make that mistake again. He looked me in the eyes and apologized. I coldly looked back at him and stated, "I have enough apologies to spread across the world, just don't do it again." Afterwards I walked away and got dressed for work.

My cousin Rachel was at my house promptly at 4:30pm just like she said she'd be. She was in a van with about four or five other people. I naturally assumed the older guy who was driving was the supervisor because he was giving us the details of the job duties we were to perform tonight. We went to approximately 7 different clinics in three different parishes. All the clinic sizes varied. A couple of the clinics had about 10 doctor offices, while another had maybe about thirty. When I made it home about 1:30am, Casey was waiting up for me and he was not pleased. He asked why I was gone so long.

"The job took that long," I stated.

"Well you can't work no more!" he whined. I politely kissed Casey on the forehead and said, "Bae, I'm grown. Who's going to stop me?" I walked away, took my bath, climbed in bed and went to sleep.

I was having trouble with CJ again because he wanted to be with his daddy. I got dressed and asked my neighbor Ms. Phyllis to keep an eye on my other three kids, while I granted CJ his wish. When we made it to Ms. Lynn's, I asked if Charles was home in the back.

"Yeah, he's home," she answered. In a matter of seconds the Duke clan were all out in the front yard and Charles comes out ranting and raving like a lunatic and talking crazy to me in front of Star and her kids, too. "Our son wants to be with you, I don't understand what the problem is", I calmly stated.

"Well, I can't take him," Charles screamed.

I snatched my son by his chin, lifting his face up towards mine and said, "See? Your Pa don't want you. Let's go!" and we turned and started walking toward the bus stop. While we are half a block from the bus stop, Charles came screaming and stomping up the block trying to catch up with me.

When he finally reached me, he gave me a thousand excuses why he can't take his son. He went to grab me and I pulled my pocket knife out. He used our son as a shield to keep me from stabbing him. That's the sign of a true bitch. I told him if I really wanted to cut him, I could go through his son if necessary. Then he tried to rush me to get the knife out of my hand. The only thing he was truly successful at was spraining my right thumb, which bothers me still today. While CJ and I were on board the bus, he continued to whine for his daddy. I told my son to remain seated and to ride the bus back to his daddy's place, then I exited and transferred to the next bus to get home. When I got to the house and told Casey what happened, he wasn't mad or upset. He just wished I wouldn't have gone, but he was glad I came back with only a sprained thumb.

The following week when I got the SSI check I received for Chadrick, I took my kids shopping for new sneakers and clothing because they had excellent report cards and they deserved it. After the purchasing was over, they wanted to go see their big brother CJ. I explained to them that I didn't have enough bus fare for all of us to go to Ms. Lynn's place, but we could walk. I told them, it would be like taking a long journey and I could buy all of them snacks on the way. They loved the idea of going on an adventure; so after dropping the rest of their things off back at the house we were on our way. It took us about two and a half hours to walk from our home to Ms. Lynn's spot. Once there, the kids had this sudden burst of energy that was so loving when they saw their sibling who by the way looked like a vagabond. He was thrilled to see them and was momentarily excited by the thought that I came bearing gifts for him in the form of new clothes and sneakers, too. When he realized it was not so, the look on his face broke my heart. However, I was determined to play the role of a stubborn parent. I decided to let him live with the choice he made in leaving home to live with his unreliable daddy. After letting the kids visit for a few hours, we made our long trek back home in fashionable time. I hurt knowing that I had to leave my first baby behind. I prayed he would desire to return to the nest soon, where he belonged, because he was truly missed. I loved my son dearly, but I just didn't want to be the cause of his unhappiness.

I worked every night, including weekends, for 10 to 12 hours sometimes. I was ecstatic when payday finally came. Upon receiving and cashing my check, I went and rented a large one bed one bath apartment with a balcony and driveway. I knew it would be my kids' dream home because it was directly across the street from a McDonald's. I also went to one of Harry's rent to own furniture stores and got me a bedroom set, and had it delivered to the apt the same day I had the utilities turned on. When the kids eventually saw and moved into the apartment, they were very happy and pleased. I knew that having the balcony and being across the street from McDonald's were extra added touches that would keep them safe and content.

In a matter of a couple of months, I managed to become an assistant supervisor for the medical clinics we were cleaning, and had been entrusted with the company van. I was so proud of myself. Mr. Luke, who was my supervisor, also became a very good friend to me. When he received a private contract to clean a day spa, he hired me as a personal assistant to work alongside him and his best friend, Mr. Pete. It seemed as if I was beginning to writing a new chapter in my life and I couldn't wait to see what all it had to tell. I had been living in my new place less than a month when I started receiving visits from Sunshine, Herman and his girlfriend Lola. It was a joy seeing them from time to time, but it wasn't long after that that Charles paid me an unexpected visit, too. He expressed how nice the apartment looked and stated he was proud of me, along with other little compliments that I suspected were hinting up to something he wanted in particular. I just had to wait for it.

My children were enjoying summer and their freedom. They had babysitters who watched them from afar, while I worked my long hours to provide and care for them. I started having disturbing dreams, or should I say visions of death and chaos again. I had been working so hard, I hadn't had the time to partake in the usual bible studies with my kids, which had become customary in our household. Realizing this made me a little depressed, but I did fret because I was convinced that prayer was going to fix that.

Just like I figured, Charles was making routine guess appearances at my house. I was not shocked when he showed up to my house with his clothes to take a shower like we were best buddies or something, but he never popped up with funds to help with the kids. These un-invited and unannounced visits of his were beginning to leave a bad taste in my mouth. The day came when I got a special visit from Casey as well; he just couldn't stay away, either. However, he came bearing gifts which to me, didn't make much of a difference. On that evening, I couldn't quite understand why I began to feel so gloomy. It caused me great alarm, so I packed my kids up and brought them to work with me that night. Casey tagged along, too. As the night went on, my babies made me feel so much better, but after I dropped Casey off at home and made my way back toward my residence that feeling of dread came back. The next day was payday again and it was time to make yet another move.

I normally would cash my check, get my kids McDonald's and drop it off to them, then head straight out to work, but not that day. Instead, I went and found another place for us to live, picked them up from home, went to McDonald's, then went to work, taking them with me. During the weekend, I and my children moved into a two bedroom duplex near the dream house that Charles abandoned me and my kids in a few years prior. It was partly furnished and we had everything required to make life as blissful as we desired. I had only a mattress on the floor, my children had bunk beds and we owned a 19 inch black and white TV, but we were truly satisfied and content.

It was awesome seeing my children really enjoying themselves as they were going to and from school, coming home laughing and so full of life without a care in the world. Knowing that I was making it all possible for them was exhilarating and meaningful to me as a per-son. The visions of chaos and death that I dreamed of so vividly had slowly began to fade. Out of nowhere, it abruptly appeared without ceasing, affecting me both during the day and the night. I never felt a wave of fear so fierce before and this left me trembling and shaken up deep down inside. I didn't understand what was going on with me, but I couldn't afford to allow my children to see the terror I felt.

The morning arrived when I was just making it inside from walking the kids to school when I heard this faint knock on the door. Barely making it to my bedroom, I turned around and returned to the entrance of my home and answered the knock in a pleasant mood. When I opened the door I didn't see anyone right away, I thought my ears must have deceived me and was about to close the door once more when a hand stopped me and I heard an all too familiar voice say, "NO MATTER WHERE YOU GO, I'LL ALWAYS FIND YOU!" He snickered, then disappeared around the corner from the house. It was at that moment that the frightful vision I had endured for close to six months was fulfilled.

I'm scared. I'm lost. The turmoil that once was deep inside of me is surrounding me now because I'm locked away inside of myself. Who are these four precious faces that call me Mama? I don't recognize them or know their names, but they are so beautiful. Can I be so deserving of such beauty that the four of these adorable little humans possess? Where am I? Time is standing still and I can't go forward or backwards, nor side to side. The darkness has swallowed me whole and I need the light, but the quiet has consumed my soul. I need to escape this wretchedness, but how? I don't know how to begin to live because my life is void of recognition. I can see a glimpse now and I can even hear a little. Is that I? I'm a child that is small and unkempt out in the dirt, shooting marbles with a smile brighter than the sun, yet I'm hungry and in need of a bath. I hear the laughter of others, but I can't join in because they're laughing at me, but why? I didn't choose this for my life. I had desires once. I wanted to be a white ballerina that was famous all over the world. Everywhere I'd go, people would rise and congratulate me for a great performance. Instead, I am locked away feeling this man penetrate my tiny rectum with a force so fierce that the mighty gust of hurricane Betsy couldn't equal his thrust. I want to scream, but I resist because I will never be called weak; no not ever.

Yet I'm here, tucked away from every sound and sight that doesn't know I'm lost inside of me. I can't comprehend whether or not I'm safe here within myself. Can I be saved? I am uncertain. I'm struggling and wrestling with this thing that I can't describe, but it knows me and me, it. It challenges me to abort all claims to my sanity and I am giving it a lot of thought. Wait, these beautiful faces seem to need me, but why? Can the man that hit me in the forehead with his knuckle be satisfied with what I have done before I collapsed within myself? I just don't know. I got to get help, where do I go? Which way do I turn? The fog is so thick in my mind I can't decipher my left from my right. How did I get here?

It was him. He found me and now I'm broken. I'm so tired. I have ran for so long, I'm exhausted and so depleted. Have I gone mad? Have I really gone mad? I can't really say. I'm not here, can't these little ones see? I'm only the shell of who they think I am. I'm so sorry, Young Ones. I can't handle the pressures of this thing that has trapped my mind and seeking a way to take my soul. What do I do? What do I do? What are the names of these four precious faces? If only I could remember. I remember mimicking the popular girls in school because it seemed I was repulsive to so many. No one understood I loved giving unto others as a way to save a piece of myself for later. I often fabricated stories while growing up because the truth was just too harsh.

I feel Him, I see Him, and I hear Him, no matter where I am or what I do. He's always existed, but His presence has abandon me at the moment. What do I do? I know He's disappointed in me and I'm ashamed because of it. My GOD who has gifted me with so much is disappointed in me. Oh my GOD! I'm so sorry. I don't deserve life. That's why he has found me and I've lost myself. He'll love them and care for them…him whose name I can't speak. They are so beautiful, these four precious faces. The soundless black atmosphere is where I'll dwell until, I can't rightfully say. I'm scared, I'm lost, and I'm alone. There are no birds here nor are there trees. No rivers, no fresh air to breathe. No caring voices, no select food choices. The air is gloom, no flowers that bloom, no not here. The darkness is King, I remember *every bad thing. No laughter to hear, only my deepest fears, that's what's here. Confusion leaves me hopeless and I feel so useless. Love never cradle me as a child, I searched many the miles, that's what I see here. I don't think I'm going to survive this time. I was born a fighter, but the fighter is dying. Who's going to save me? Those four beautiful faces can't recognize real death; they see me as I was hours ago, not as I am now. I'm barely visible to me so I know the world can't see me. My eyes are open and I see not. My ears are open and I hear not, I'm on the edge of something and I don't know where it will take me. I have a glimpse of hell before me and behind me, I guess I got to see this thing through... whatever it is. I'm not sure how long I'm going to be here, stuck in the place called **Nowhere** but I got to find my way out to see the fate of these four precious faces.*

I was handcuffed in the back of a squad car. Now I am strapped down to a narrow bed surrounded by four white padded walls. The people in the room are carefully whispering about me. Now I'm alone. I can't move or think. My focus is on the clock in the upper left corner of the room. Is it daytime or nighttime? I don't know. I think I'll sleep now. Yes, sleep sounds really good.

TO BE CONTINUED...